HARRY POTTER AND THE SORCERER'S STONE

J. K. Rowling

TECHNICAL DIRECTOR Maxwell Krohn
EDITORIAL DIRECTOR Justin Kestler
MANAGING EDITOR Ben Florman

SERIES EDITORS Boomie Aglietti, Justin Kestler
PRODUCTION Christian Lorentzen, Camille Murphy

WRITERS Ari Weinstein, John Henriksen
EDITOR Boomie Aglietti

This edition published by Spark Publishing

Spark Publishing
A Division of SparkNotes LLC
120 Fifth Avenue, 8th Floor
New York, NY 10011

02 03 04 05 SN 9 8 7 6 5 4 3 2 1

Please send all comments and questions or report errors to
feedback@sparknotes.com.

Library of Congress information available upon request

Printed and bound in the United States

RRD-C

ISBN 1-58663-518-2

INTRODUCTION: STOPPING TO BUY SPARKNOTES ON A SNOWY EVENING

Whose words these are you *think* you know.
Your paper's due tomorrow, though;
We're glad to see you stopping here
To get some help before you go.

Lost your course? You'll find it here.
Face tests and essays without fear.
Between the words, good grades at stake:
Get great results throughout the year.

Once school bells caused your heart to quake
As teachers circled each mistake.
Use SparkNotes and no longer weep,
Ace every single test you take.

Yes, books are lovely, dark, and deep,
But only what you grasp you keep,
With hours to go before you sleep,
With hours to go before you sleep.

CONTENTS

NOTE: This SparkNote refers to the 1999 Scholastic paperback edition of *Harry Potter and the Sorcerer's Stone*. The book was originally published in 1997 in the United Kingdom as *Harry Potter and the Philosopher's Stone*.

Context

ARRY POTTER AND THE SORCERER'S STONE emerged from the creative mind of J. K. (Joanna Kathleen) Rowling on a train ride from Manchester to London in 1990. Rowling was a single mother of an infant daughter and living on welfare in Edinburgh, Scotland, when she began the novel. Putting pen to paper in a café while her baby, Jessica, napped, Rowling soon skyrocketed to fame and fortune. While she received an advance of only £2,500 (approximately $3,500 American) for the novel from her British publisher, Bloomsbury, she has since become one of the richest women in the United Kingdom. Her first book was published under the original title *Harry Potter and the Philosopher's Stone* (the book's American publishers feared that mention of philosophers would scare away young readers and changed the title to *Harry Potter and the Sorcerer's Stone*). The book garnered rave reviews in the United Kingdom, where it won the British Book Award's Children's Book of the Year prize, as well as the Smarties Book Prize. Critics have compared her to classic children's writers such as Roald Dahl, C. S. Lewis, and J. R. R. Tolkien, who also fused the traditional adventure story with fantastic elements drawn from myth and legend.

Soon after the British release of *Harry Potter and the Philosopher's Stone*, Arthur Levine, an editorial director for Scholastic Books, bought the American rights to the novel for the impressive sum of $105,000. This money allowed Rowling to retire from a teaching job and devote herself entirely to writing. When it was released in America, *Harry Potter and the Sorcerer's Stone* almost immediately became a publishing sensation, holding the top spot on the New York Times Best-Seller List for several months. The book was unique in attracting both young and adult readers; indeed, the British publisher issued an edition with a less colorful cover for grown-ups to read on trains without having to hide the novel behind a newspaper. Spurred by the success of her first book, Rowling produced a number of sequels, which have won the Smarties Book Prize so often (in three consecutive years) that Rowling has requested that her books no longer be considered candidates for the prize. To date, the Harry Potter empire includes four books in the Potter series, a couple of related works written by Rowling for charity (*Quidditch*

Through the Ages and *Fantastical Beasts and Where to Find Them*), and a major motion picture produced by Warner Brothers.

Harry Potter and the Sorcerer's Stone draws on a long tradition of English fantasy works that seem to be for children but are in fact deep allegories of the human condition. Rowling herself has stated that her book is really about imagination and that practicing wizardry is only a metaphor for developing one's full potential. On one level, the story is a thriller with a criminal plot (the planned theft of the Sorcerer's Stone) that is thwarted by a group of brave students, just as C. S. Lewis's Narnia books—childhood favorites of Rowling's—are about children who explore a strange land and perform heroic deeds. But on a deeper level, *Harry Potter and the Sorcerer's Stone,* like the Narnia books, illustrates the challenges and adventures of growing up. Rowling's book outlines every child's ordeal of becoming an individual, winning respect from peers, learning about loyalty, discovering the difference between forgivable vices and unforgivable sins, and believing in something bigger than oneself. Harry's transformation from a forgotten orphan living under the stairs into a publicly recognized individual (symbolized by the magical, adultlike letters addressed to him), and then finally into a renowned hero represents the successful entry into the public world wished for by every child. Harry's escape from misery to a new place where he has friends, respect, and a useful role in the world is a projection of every child's ideal life. Most important, Harry's discovery that there is something uniquely valuable inside him represents the dream of innumerable people—children and adults alike—who enjoy indulging their imaginations.

PLOT OVERVIEW

MR. DURSLEY, A WELL-OFF ENGLISHMAN, notices strange happenings on his way to work one day. That night, Albus Dumbledore, the head of a wizardry academy called Hogwarts, meets Professor McGonagall, who also teaches at Hogwarts, and a giant named Hagrid outside the Dursley home. Dumbledore tells McGonagall that someone named Voldemort has killed a Mr. and Mrs. Potter and tried unsuccessfully to kill their baby son, Harry. Dumbledore leaves Harry with an explanatory note in a basket in front of the Dursley home.

Ten years later, the Dursley household is dominated by the Dursleys' son, Dudley, who torments and bullies Harry. Dudley is spoiled, while Harry is forced to sleep in a cupboard under the stairs. At the zoo on Dudley's birthday, the glass in front of a boa constrictor exhibit disappears, frightening everyone. Harry is later punished for this incident.

Mysterious letters begin arriving for Harry. They worry Mr. Dursley, who tries to keep them from Harry, but the letters keep arriving through every crack in the house. Finally, he flees with his family to a secluded island shack on the eve of Harry's eleventh birthday. At midnight, they hear a large bang on the door and Hagrid enters. Hagrid hands Harry an admissions letter to the Hogwarts School of Witchcraft and Wizardry. Harry learns that the Dursleys have tried to deny Harry's wizardry all these years.

The next day, Hagrid takes Harry to London to shop for school supplies. First they go to the wizard bank, Gringotts, where Harry learns that his parents have left him a hefty supply of money. They shop on the wizards' commercial street known as Diagon Alley, where Harry is fitted for his school uniform. Harry buys books, ingredients for potions, and, finally, a magic wand—the companion wand to the evil Voldemort's.

A month later, Harry goes to the train station and catches his train to Hogwarts on track nine and three quarters. On the train, Harry befriends other first-year students like Ron Weasley and Hermione Granger, a Muggle girl chosen to attend Hogwarts. At school, the first-years take turns putting on the "Sorting Hat" to find out in which residential house they will live. Harry fears being assigned to the sinister Slytherin house, but he, Ron, and Hermione end up in the noble Gryffindor house.

As the school year gets underway, Harry discovers that his Potions professor, Snape, does not like him. Hagrid reassures Harry that Snape has no reason to dislike him. During their first flying lesson on broomsticks, the students are told to stay grounded while the teacher takes an injured boy named Neville to the hospital. Draco Malfoy, a Slytherin bully, snatches Neville's prized toy and flies off with it to the top of a tree. Harry flies after him. Malfoy throws the ball in the air, and Harry speeds downward, making a spectacular catch. Professor McGonagall witnesses this incident. Instead of punishing Harry, she recommends that he play Quidditch, a much-loved game that resembles soccer played on broomsticks, for Gryffindor. Later that day, Malfoy challenges Harry to a wizard's duel at midnight. Malfoy doesn't show up at the appointed place, and Harry almost gets in trouble. While trying to hide, he accidentally discovers a fierce three-headed dog guarding a trapdoor in the forbidden third-floor corridor.

On Halloween, a troll is found in the building. The students are all escorted back to their dormitories, but Harry and Ron sneak off to find Hermione, who is alone and unaware of the troll. Unwittingly, they lock the troll in the girls' bathroom along with Hermione. Together, they defeat the troll. Hermione tells a lie to protect Harry and Ron from being punished. During Harry's first Quidditch match, his broom jerks out of control. Hermione notices Snape staring at Harry and muttering a curse. She concludes that he is jinxing Harry's broom, and she sets Snape's clothes on fire. Harry regains control of the broom and makes a spectacular play to win the Quidditch match.

For Christmas, Harry receives his father's invisibility cloak, and he explores the school, unseen, late at night. He discovers the Mirror of Erised, which displays the deepest desire of whoever looks in it. Harry looks in it and sees his parents alive. After Christmas, Harry, Ron, and Hermione begin to unravel the mysterious connection between a break-in at Gringotts and the three-headed guard dog. They learn that the dog is guarding the Sorcerer's Stone, which is capable of providing eternal life and unlimited wealth to its owner and belongs to Nicolas Flamel, Dumbledore's old partner.

A few weeks later, Hagrid wins a dragon egg in a poker game. Because it is illegal to own dragons, Harry, Ron, and Hermione contact Ron's older brother, who studies dragons. They arrange to get rid of the dragon but get caught. Harry, Ron, and Hermione are severely punished, and Gryffindor is docked 150 points. Furthermore, part of their punishment is to go into the enchanted forest with Hagrid to find out who has been killing unicorns recently. In the forest, Harry comes upon a hooded man drinking unicorn blood. The man tries to attack Harry, but Harry is rescued by a friendly centaur who tells him that his assailant was Voldemort. Harry also learns that it is Voldemort who has been trying to steal the Sorcerer's Stone.

Harry decides that he must find the stone before Voldemort does. He, Ron, and Hermione sneak off that night to the forbidden third-floor corridor. They get past the guard dog and perform many impressive feats as they get closer and closer to the stone. Harry ultimately finds himself face to face with Quirrell, who announces that Harry must die. Knowing that Harry desires to find the stone, Quirrell puts Harry in front of the Mirror of Erised and makes him state what he sees. Harry sees himself with the stone in his pocket, and at that same moment he actually feels it in his pocket. But he tells Quirrell that he sees something else. A voice tells Quirrell that the boy is lying and requests to speak to Harry face to face. Quirrell removes his turban and reveals Voldemort's face on the back of his head. Voldemort, who is inhabiting Quirrell's body, instructs Quirrell to kill Harry, but Quirrell is burned by contact with the boy. A struggle ensues and Harry passes out.

When Harry regains consciousness, he is in the hospital with Dumbledore. Dumbledore explains that he saved Harry from Quirrell just in time. He adds that he and Flamel have decided to destroy the stone. Harry heads down to the end-of-year banquet, where Slytherin is celebrating its seventh consecutive win of the house championship cup. Dumbledore gets up and awards many last-minute points to Gryffindor for the feats of Harry and his friends, winning the house cup for Gryffindor. Harry returns to London to spend the summer with the Dursleys.

Character List

Harry Potter The protagonist of the story, who is gradually transformed from timid weakling to powerful hero by the end. Marked on the forehead with a lightning-shaped scar, Harry is marked also by the confrontation between good and bad magic that caused that scar: the standoff between the evil Voldemort and his parents who died to save their son. The story eventually becomes a tale of Harry's vengeance for their wrongful deaths. As he matures, he shows himself to be caring and shrewd, a loyal friend, and an excellent Quidditch player.

Hermione Granger Initially an annoying goody-two-shoes who studies too much and obeys the school rules too zealously. Hermione eventually becomes friendly with Harry after she learns to value friendship over perfectionism and obedience. She comes from a purely Muggle family, and her character illustrates the social-adjustment problems often faced by new students at Hogwarts.

Ron Weasley A shy, modest boy who comes from an impoverished wizard family. Ron is Harry's first friend at Hogwarts, and they become close. He lacks Harry's gusto and charisma, but his loyalty and help are useful to Harry throughout their adventures. Ron's mediocrity despite his wizard background reminds us that success at Hogwarts is based solely on talent and hard work, not on family connections. Ron's willingness to be beaten up by the monstrous chess queen shows how selfless and generous he is.

Hagrid   An oafish giant who works as a groundskeeper at Hogwarts. Rubeus Hagrid is a well-meaning creature with more kindness than brains. He cares deeply for Harry, as evidenced by the tears he sheds upon having to leave the infant Harry with the Dursleys. His fondness for animals is endearing, even if it gets him into trouble (as when he tries raising a dragon at home). Hagrid symbolizes the importance of generosity and human warmth in a world menaced by conniving villains.

Albus Dumbledore The kind, wise head of Hogwarts. Though he is a famous wizard, Dumbledore is as humble and adorable as his name suggests. While other school officials, such as Professor McGonagall, are obsessed with the rules, Dumbledore respects them (as his warnings against entering the Forbidden Forest remind us) but does not exaggerate their importance. He appears to have an almost superhuman level of wisdom, knowledge, and personal understanding, and it seems that he may have set up the whole quest for the Sorcerer's Stone so that Harry could prove himself.

Voldemort A great wizard gone bad. When he killed Harry's parents, Voldemort gave Harry a lightning-shaped scar. Voldemort has thus shaped Harry's life so that Harry's ultimate destruction of him appears as a kind of vengeance. Voldemort, whose name in French means either "flight of death" or "theft of death," is associated both with high-flying magic and with deceit throughout the story. He is determined to escape death by finding the Sorcerer's Stone. Voldemort's weak point is that he cannot understand love, and thus cannot touch Harry's body, which still bears the traces of Harry's mother's love for her son.

Draco Malfoy An arrogant student and Harry's nemesis. Malfoy, whose name translates roughly to "dragon of bad faith," is a rich snob from a long line of wizards who feels entitled to the Hogwarts experience. He makes fun of the poorer Ron Weasley and advises Harry to choose his friends more carefully. As the story progresses, Malfoy becomes more and more inimical to Harry and his friends, and there is a hint that he may grow up to become another Voldemort.

Neville Longbottom A timid Hogwarts classmate of Harry's. Neville is friendly and loyal, but like Ron, he lacks Harry's charisma. Like Hermione, he is initially too obedient, and when the time comes to go after the Sorcerer's Stone, he fears punishment and threatens to report his friends to the teachers.

Professor McGonagall The head of Gryffindor House at Hogwarts and a high-ranking woman in the wizard world. Minerva McGonagall is fair but extremely stern and severe in her punishments. Her devotion to the letter of the law is impressive but a bit cold, and we constantly feel that she could never become a warm and wise figure like Dumbledore. Rowling named her after a notoriously bad nineteenth-century Scottish poet named William McGonagall who was nevertheless highly confident of his own talents.

Professor Snape A professor of Potions at Hogwarts. Severus Snape dislikes Harry and appears to be an evil man for most of the story. His name associates him not only with unfair snap judgments of others but also with his violent intentions to snap the bones of his enemies. Snape's grudge against Harry, which is nevertheless far from a murderous ill will, helps us remember the difference between forgivable vices and unforgivable evil intentions.

Professor Quirrell A stuttering and seemingly harmless man, and a professor of Defense against the Dark Arts at Hogwarts. Quirrell appears as nervous and squirrelly as his name suggests for most of the story. It is he, for example, who nearly faints when announcing the news that a troll is loose in the school. It turns out later, however, that Quirrell has faked his withdrawing meekness and is actually a cold-blooded conniver.

Vernon Dursley Harry's rich uncle, with whom Harry lives for ten miserable years. Dursley symbolizes the Muggle world at its most silly and mediocre. It is through Mr. Dursley's jaded Muggle eyes that we first glimpse wizards, and his closed-mindedness toward the colorful cloaks and literate cats that he meets emphasizes how different the human and wizard worlds are.

Petunia Dursley Mr. Dursley's wife. Petunia is an overly doting mother to her spoiled son, Dudley, and a prison-keeper to Harry. She is haughty and excessively concerned with what the neighbors think of her family. She is somewhat humanized for us when we discover that she was always jealous of the magical gifts of her sister, Lily, Harry's witch mother. Perhaps her malevolence toward Harry springs from an earlier resentment of her sister.

Dudley Dursley Harry's cousin, a spoiled, fat bully. Annoying and loud, Dudley manipulates parental love to get what he wants—his outrageous desires for multiple television sets foreshadow the important scenes involving the Mirror of Erised and the wrongful desire for eternal life that motivates Voldemort. Dudley's tormenting of Harry foreshadows Malfoy's later bullying tendencies at Hogwarts, though he is less gifted than Malfoy.

ANALYSIS OF MAJOR CHARACTERS

HARRY POTTER

Harry Potter is the hero of the story. Orphaned as a baby, he is brought up by his aunt and uncle, the Dursleys, maltreated by them, and tormented by their obnoxious son, Dudley. Neglected and disdained, Harry grows up to be a timid boy unsure of his abilities. His sudden fame as a wizard at Hogwarts comes not just as a total contrast to his earlier forgotten misery, but as a fate that we feel is very much deserved after his youthful suffering. Yet even after he becomes famous, Harry never loses his modesty and humility. Even by the end of the story, when he has obtained the Sorcerer's Stone and saved Hogwarts (and perhaps the whole world) from Voldemort, Harry does not revel in his success. He simply asks Dumbledore a few factual questions and is satisfied with the answers, never expecting any praise. Moreover, he does not wish to use his powers to fulfill grandiose wishes. Dumbledore wisely knows that, unlike Voldemort, Harry will desire only to get the magic stone, not to use it. He does not covet riches or power, or harbor any secret wild ambition; he just wants to make sure that the stone and its power do not fall into the wrong hands. The simplicity of his desire is part of what makes him a hero.

Harry's capacity for loyal friendship is another of his attractive features. It is also one of the surest proofs that Harry is developing at Hogwarts, where he is a lonely individual at the story's beginning but has a circle of loyal friends and admirers by the end. His faithful membership in Gryffindor is a symbol of his newly developing team spirit. He prefers maintaining good relations with his schoolmates to basking in individual glory. Similarly, rather than boast of his immense talent at Quidditch, he rejoices in the communal victory for his house and does not stop for applause even when he breaks Quidditch records. He is willing to put himself at risk for the sake of a friend, sometimes foolishly, as when he battles a troll to save Hermione and when he gets himself severely punished for helping Hagrid with his dragon. Harry's success at forging true friendships and overcoming his early loneliness is almost as inspiring as his defeat of the evil and powerful Voldemort.

DRACO MALFOY

The son of a long line of wizards, Malfoy is the opposite of Harry in his familiarity with the Hogwarts experience, his sense of entitlement, his snobbery, and his generally unpleasant character. Rowling includes Malfoy in the story partly as a foil to Harry's character; in seeing how unlikable Malfoy is, we appreciate all the more Harry's kindness and generosity of spirit. For example, right after Malfoy insults Ron's poverty on the train ride to Hogwarts, Harry buys double the number of pastries that he needs and shares them with Ron. Malfoy's snobbish insistence on only socializing with children of the best families, his selfishness, and his overwhelming aura of superiority all resemble similar characteristics in Dudley Dursley, Harry's nemesis in the Muggle world. The similarity between Malfoy and Dudley is important in reminding us that Harry's new life will not be an escape from his old problems. Malfoy's presence throughout the preparatory stages of Harry's educational adventure is a rude awakening to the realities of the wizards' world, which includes detestable characters like Malfoy. At Hogwarts, Harry will not be surrounded simply by kindness, but will have to face unpleasantness as well, just as he has earlier in his life.

But Malfoy also plays a somewhat deeper role in the story, at least symbolically. He is mean-spirited and nasty, but there are hints that in time he may become far worse than nasty; he may blossom into a truly evil character like Voldemort. The Latin word *draco* means "dragon," and the French words *mal* and *foi* mean "bad faith." We sometimes suspect that Draco Malfoy may indeed be a "bad faith dragon," a monster of ill will. Perhaps he is a dragon still being incubated, like Hagrid's baby dragon that will soon grow into a destructive monster. Malfoy belongs to the darkly powerful house of Slytherin, as did Voldemort. His total lack of redeeming features makes him almost as flat a villain as Voldemort. Like Voldemort, Malfoy is not so much a realistic character as a caricature of badness. Of course, we do not know what Malfoy will become in the future. But his presence at Hogwarts reminds us that every generation will have its heroes and its villains, and that the struggle between right and wrong will always continue.

HERMIONE GRANGER

Hermione's character develops significantly over the course of the story and sheds light on Harry's character as well. At the outset, she is an annoying perfectionist, a goody-two-shoes who has read all the books for her classes in advance, has learned all about Hogwarts, and never breaks the rules. When she first speaks to Harry on the train ride to school, she is eager to impress him with her knowledge, whereas Harry only wants to make friends. Her intellectual talents are indeed worthy of pride, as we find out later when she scores 112 percent on her final exam. But we sense that her show-off side is a defense against her feelings of inferiority, because she comes from a Muggle family and, like Harry, is unfamiliar with the wizard world. In both Hermione and Harry we see that learning wizardry requires a great deal of social adjustment and self-confidence.

Hermione's development into a likable character and a friend begins in the troll episode, when Harry and Ron are reprimanded for trying to save her from the monster and she coolly delivers a bold-faced lie to the teacher. The little girl who has been abiding by all the school rules now dares to lie to her superiors, and a new friendship is born. Hermione's decision to support her friends rather than obey the rules showcases what is perhaps truly valuable about Harry's Hogwarts experience. The school teaches him not just facts from books and how to follow procedures, but also—and perhaps more important—loyalty, compassion for others, and solidarity.

CHARACTER ANALYSIS

THEMES, MOTIFS & SYMBOLS

THEMES

Themes are the fundamental and often universal ideas explored in a literary work.

THE VALUE OF HUMILITY

Harry Potter and the Sorcerer's Stone emphasizes the virtue of humility by showcasing the extraordinary modesty of its hero and by making this modesty an important part of Harry's success in obtaining the Sorcerer's Stone. Harry's humility is no doubt ingrained in him during his ten miserable years of neglect and cruelty with the Dursleys. But Harry does not stop being humble when he gains fame, wealth, and popularity at Hogwarts. His reaction to the discovery that everyone seems to know his name on the train to Hogwarts does not make him primp and pose, but rather only makes him hope that he can manage to live up to his reputation. In this respect, he contrasts sharply with Draco Malfoy, who prides himself on his family reputation and downplays achievement.

Similarly, when it becomes apparent that Harry has an astounding gift for Quidditch, his reaction is not to glory in his superstar abilities, but rather to practice more industriously than before. When Harry breaks Quidditch records by catching the Golden Snitch in the first five minutes of the game, he does not even pause to appreciate the applause of the crowd, but rushes off. Harry's refusal to glorify himself is instrumental in getting the stone because he differs from wicked wizards like Quirrell in that he desires only to find the Stone for the common good, not to use it to acquire personal fame or fortune. If Harry were less humble, he would be unable to seize the stone. He is the extreme opposite of Voldemort, who strives only to achieve his own selfish goals.

THE OCCASIONAL NECESSITY OF REBELLION

Hogwarts is a well-run institution, with clearly spelled out rules that are strictly enforced. Midlevel teachers and school administrators like Professor McGonagall constantly police students for violations, and the rules are taken seriously. Even at the highest level of the Hogwarts administration, there is a clear respect for the rules. Dumbledore is a stern taskmaster. He makes a very gentle and warm welcome speech to the first-year students, but he throws in a few menacing reminders about the prohibition of visits to the Forbidden Forest and the third-floor corridor. None of these Hogwarts rules ever seems arbitrary or unfair. On the contrary, we generally approve of them, feeling that in a world imperiled by misused magic, strict control over student behavior is necessary.

Even so, it soon becomes clear that Harry is unable to abide perfectly by the rules. He enters the third-floor corridor in the full knowledge that it is forbidden territory, and he dons the invisibility cloak to inspect the restricted-books section of the library. After the flying instructor has clearly prohibited broomstick flying until she returns, Harry does not hesitate to take off after Malfoy to retrieve Neville's stolen toy. And Harry approves of infractions of the rules by others as well. When Hagrid reveals that he is engaged in an illegal dragon-rearing endeavor, Harry not only fails to report Hagrid to the authorities, but actually helps Hagrid with the dragon.

Harry's occasional rebellions against the rules are not vices or failings. Rather, they enhance his heroism because they show that he is able to think for himself and make his own judgments. The contrast to Harry in this respect is the perfectionist Hermione, who never breaks a rule at the beginning and who is thus annoying to both Harry and us. When she eventually lies to a teacher, showing that she too can transcend the rules, Hermione becomes Harry's friend. One of the main lessons of the story is that while rules are good and necessary, sometimes it is necessary to question and even break them for the right reasons.

THE DANGERS OF DESIRE

As the pivotal importance of the desire-reflecting Mirror of Erised reveals, learning what to want is an important part of one's development. Excessive desire is condemned from the story's beginning, as the spoiled Dudley's outrageous demands for multiple television sets appear foolish and obnoxious. The same type of greed appears later in a much more evil form in the power-hungry desires of Voldemort, who pursues the Sorcerer's Stone's promise of unlimited wealth and life. While Voldemort and Dudley are obviously different in other respects, they share an uncontrollable desire that repels

Harry and makes him the enemy of both of them. Desire is not necessarily wrong or bad, as Dumbledore explains to Harry before the Mirror of Erised—Harry's desire to see his parents alive is touching and noble. But overblown desire is dangerous in that it can make people lose perspective on life, which is why Dumbledore advises Harry not to seek out the mirror again. Dumbledore himself illustrates the power and grandeur of one who has renounced desires almost completely when he says that all he wants is a pair of warm socks. This restraint is the model for Harry's own development in the story.

MOTIFS

Motifs are recurring structures, contrasts, or literary devices that can help to develop and inform the text's major themes.

MUGGLES

The world of the Muggles, or ordinary, nonmagical human beings, is an obvious contrast to the realm of the wizards in a variety of ways. Wizards appear grand and colorful, but Muggles are bland and conventional. The story's main representatives of the Muggle world are the Dursleys, who are cruel, closed-minded, selfish, and self-deluded. When we first encounter wizards in the story, we do so through the strongly disapproving eyes of Mr. Dursley, who is contemptuous of the wizards' emerald-green capes and purple robes. Our reaction is most likely to object to Mr. Dursley's lack of imagination, as the wizard world seems a refreshing contrast to the constraining boredom of Muggle life.

But in going off to Hogwarts, Harry does not leave behind his Muggle existence forever. The same qualities that make the Muggles objectionable are present among wizards as well. Mrs. Dursley's snobbery is fully apparent in Malfoy's snooty name-dropping, as Harry is soon disappointed to observe. Dudley's self-centered and uncaring greed is present in a more grandiose and powerful way in the evil Voldemort's greed. And Hogwarts itself is composed of students from wizard and Muggle backgrounds alike. The point of the story is not that Muggles are bad and wizards are good, or even that Muggles are boring while wizards are exciting. It is rather that the world is made up of different types of people with different aptitudes and different desires who should be able to coexist. Muggles must be free to develop into wizards if they have the gift and the calling. If they do, they can liberate themselves and find their true selves.

POINTS

One of the central aspects of life at Hogwarts is the ongoing competition for the house championship, which is determined by the greatest accumulation of points. Students accumulate points for their houses by performing particularly good actions and by winning at Quidditch, and they lose points for performing particularly bad actions. The points system thus symbolizes the need for a careful accounting of one's actions, as a careless penalty could result in a defeat for one's peers. It also shows an interesting twist on morality, as points can be earned not only for good or righteous behavior, but also for athletic excellence. Moral and spiritual achievement is rewarded but so is physical achievement. This fact brings the world of *Harry Potter and the Sorcerer's Stone* out of a Christian ethical system (in which pure intentions of the spirit matter most) and brings it closer to an ancient notion of human excellence. The word "virtue" derives from the Latin word *virtus*, which referred in ancient times to manly successes in martial and physical exploits. This quality saw the body and the soul as one entity and recognized excellence as a mixture of different kinds of achievement. Harry, with his mental and physical prowess, embodies this ancient quality.

AUTHORITY

Both admirable and bogus versions of authority pop up throughout the story. Bogus authority first appears in the figures of Mr. and Mrs. Dursley, who order Harry around with no sense of appropriateness. Their authority is based solely on power: they are the adults, with financial and physical superiority over children, and in their minds they feel entitled to treat Harry like a slave. But we see the emptiness and limits of Mr. Dursley's authority as soon as the wizard world makes its appearance. Mr. Dursley is suddenly unable to control even the mail that arrives at his house. His power vanishes completely and with it so does his authority. By the time he flees to the shack on the island with his family, he has become a ridiculous figure, desperately clinging on to an idea of control that he lacks utterly. Even the uncouth and oafish Hagrid, who appears on the island, has more authority than Mr. Dursley. By the end of the story, Dumbledore emerges as the true authority figure. Dumbledore has immense power but does not use it. When he wants Harry to stop visiting the Mirror of Erised, he recommends that Harry stop going instead of ordering him to stop. Based on wisdom and kindness rather than raw power, Dumbledore's model of authority becomes Harry's own.

SYMBOLS

Symbols are objects, characters, figures, or colors used to represent abstract ideas or concepts.

HARRY'S SCAR

The lightning-shaped scar that Harry receives from Voldemort symbolizes everything unique and astounding about Harry, though he never thinks twice about the scar until its history is finally told to him. Like the famous scar of Odysseus in Homer's epic poem the *Odyssey,* Harry's forehead lightning bolt is a badge of honor, an emblem of having survived a great battle and of being destined to wage still more battles in the future. It constantly connects Harry to the past, not just to the trauma of the struggle against the evil Voldemort, but also to the loving parents who tried to protect him. The scar is also a symbol of Harry's emotional sensitivity, because it hurts him whenever hatred is directed at him, as when Snape first sees him at Hogwarts or when Quirrell tries to grab him.

QUIDDITCH

As the preferred sport and pastime of the wizard world, Quidditch is entertainment, but the game is also a symbol of the deeper virtues taught at Hogwarts. The all-consuming importance of Quidditch at the school shows that magic is not just a bookish pursuit, but has a physical and practical application as well. Hermione may learn all of her textbooks perfectly, but she is not a hero for doing so; heroism is won on the Quidditch fields. Quidditch also shows that wizardry is intended for much more than the self-centered use of magic powers for personal glory. Any wizard who uses it for such ends alone is, like Voldemort, no longer a part of the team-spirit philosophy of Hogwarts. A person should use magic with an awareness of others' needs and values, just as winning at Quidditch depends on the successful interaction of several players acting cooperatively. No matter how talented a single Quidditch player like Harry might be, he or she cannot play the game alone.

The Mirror of Erised

Harry's encounter with the Mirror of Erised symbolizes his growing self-awareness, as the magic mirror forces him to look within himself and face the question of what he really wants. Harry has never had to inquire into his own desires before, because the Dursleys never cared about his desires and, upon arriving at Hogwarts, he seems to have everything he needs in his daily schedule of classes and meals. But the Hogwarts experience is meant to be more than a routine of memorizing formulas and learning to transform matches into pins. It is meant to bring personal growth and character development, for which it is necessary to examine one's soul.

Harry's desires, as reflected in the mirror, are noble ones; he wants to see his family alive and then wants to find the Sorcerer's Stone for the common good. Voldemort, on the other hand, is driven by nothing but his ego, and his desires are wholly selfish. The Mirror of Erised shows us that who we are (literally, the reflection of ourselves that we see in the mirror) is defined by what we want—our desires shape our identities. That Harry is the one who ends up with the Stone teaches us that we must temper our desires.

Summary & Analysis

Chapter 1

Summary

> *[F]or eleven years I have been trying to persuade people to call him by his proper name: Voldemort.*
>
> (See QUOTATIONS, p. 51)

The Dursleys are a well-to-do, status-conscious family living in Surrey, England. Eager to keep up proper appearances, they are embarrassed by Mrs. Dursley's eccentric sister, Mrs. Potter, whom for years Mrs. Dursley has pretended not to know. On his way to work one ordinary morning, Mr. Dursley notices a cat reading a map. He is unsettled, but tells himself that he has only imagined it. Then, as Mr. Dursley is waiting in traffic, he notices people dressed in brightly colored cloaks. Walking past a bakery later that day, he overhears people talking in an excited manner about his sister-in-law's family, the Potters, and the Potters' one-year-old son, Harry. Disturbed but still not sure anything is wrong, Mr. Dursley decides not to say anything to his wife. On the way home, he bumps into a strangely dressed man who gleefully exclaims that someone named "You-Know-Who" has finally gone and that even a "Muggle" like Mr. Dursley should rejoice. Meanwhile, the news is full of unusual reports of shooting stars and owls flying during the day.

That night, as the Dursleys are falling asleep, Albus Dumbledore, a wizard and the head of the Hogwarts wizardry academy, appears on their street. He shuts off all the streetlights and approaches a cat that is soon revealed to be a woman named Professor McGonagall (who also teaches at Hogwarts) in disguise. They discuss the disappearance of You-Know-Who, otherwise known as Voldemort. Dumbledore tells McGonagall that Voldemort killed the Potter parents the previous night and tried to kill their son, Harry, as well, but was unable to. Dumbledore adds that Voldemort's power apparently began to wane after his failed attempt to kill Harry and that he retreated. Dumbledore adds that the baby Harry can be left on the Dursleys' doorstep. McGonagall protests that Harry cannot be brought up by the Dursleys. But Dumbledore insists that there is no one else to take care of the child. He says that when Harry is old enough, he will be told of his fate. A giant named Hagrid, who is carrying a bundle of blankets with the baby Harry inside, then falls out of the sky on a motorcycle. Dumbledore takes Harry and places him on the Dursley's doorstep with an explanatory letter he has written to the Dursleys, and the three part ways.

ANALYSIS

From the outset, Rowling creates a great buzz about the protagonist of the story, Harry Potter, both for the other characters in the story and for us, the readers. She does not explain Harry's importance but simply shows how his existence affects the world. Mr. Dursley, for example, encounters all sorts of unusual occurrences—a cat reading a map, people walking around in cloaks, the giddy mention of the departure of someone called You-Know-Who. These omens create a potent aura of mystery around Harry. Additionally, though we do not yet understand why Harry is special, we see that he is destined to play an important role. Rowling situates him in opposition to the powerful and feared Voldemort, and it becomes clear that these two figures will probably confront each other at some point in a climactic battle.

The contrast that Rowling establishes between day and night prefigures the more important contrast between the story's ordinary world and its wizard world. Mr. Dursley, who walks around during the day, epitomizes the boredom and dullness of everyday life, while Albus Dumbledore, who slinks around at night, epitomizes the fantasy and mystery of wizardry. His act of magically putting out all the streetlights near the Dursleys' house creates a separation between these two realms. Professor McGonagall's ability to take the shape of both a cat and a human illustrates the difference between wizards, who have magic at their disposal, and Muggles, who do not. But Rowling soon shows us a much greater separation—a geographical one—between these two realms, carrying us eventually from an ordinary English town into the magical places that wizards frequent.

This first chapter introduces a number of elements important to the story without explaining them, stirring our curiosity and emphasizing the idea of this mysterious other world that is far away from everyday reality. The word "Muggle," for example, is used repeatedly, and though we hear it referred to humans, we do not fully understand its associations. However, even though the meaning of the word escapes us, we feel the importance of the distinction between Muggles and non-Muggles. Similarly, we feel that there is something meaningful about Harry's lightning-bolt forehead scar, though we cannot explain it any more than Harry can. Like Harry, we are forced to accept a lot of information we cannot process at first, so that we are humbled before the complexity of the wizards' world. It is important that Harry's initiation into magic is gradual so that we can identify with what he is feeling; like us, Harry is entering an unknown world.

CHAPTER 2

SUMMARY

Ten years have passed. Harry is now almost eleven and living in wretchedness in a cupboard under the stairs in the Dursley house. He is tormented by the Dursleys' son, Dudley, a spoiled and whiny boy. Harry is awakened one morning by his aunt, Petunia, telling him to tend to the bacon immediately, because it is Dudley's birthday and everything must be perfect. Dudley gets upset because he has only thirty-seven presents, one fewer than the previous year. When a neighbor calls to say she will not be able to watch Harry for the day, Dudley begins to cry, as he is upset that Harry will have to be brought along on Dudley's birthday trip to the zoo. At the zoo, the Dursleys spoil Dudley and his friend Piers, neglecting Harry as usual. In the reptile house, Harry pays close attention to a boa constrictor and is astonished when he is able to have a conversation with it. Noticing what Harry is doing, Piers calls over Mr. Dursley and Dudley, who pushes Harry aside to get a better look at the snake. At this moment, the glass front of the snake's tank vanishes and the boa constrictor slithers out onto the floor. Dudley and Piers claim that the snake attacked them. The Dursleys are in shock. At home, Harry is punished for the snake incident, being sent to his cupboard without any food, though he feels he had nothing to do with what happened.

ANALYSIS

Character names in *Harry Potter* are carefully chosen not to be life-like but rather to color our understanding of the various characters' social ranks and personalities. This technique, which the nineteenth-century English author Charles Dickens used prolifically in such novels as *Great Expectations* and *A Tale of Two Cities,* is closer to caricature than to realism and gives each character a larger-than-life, mythical feel. Harry Potter, for instance, is an ordinary and unpretentious name, though there are associations of creativity and usefulness in his last name: a potter makes pottery, which has a practical function. By contrast, the Dursleys, who brim with self-importance and snobbery, are named after a town in Gloucestershire once important in the medieval wool trade: their name suggests an old-fashioned class-conscious life that may have outlived its grandeur.

The Dursleys' first names have similar upper-class connotations. The names Dudley, Petunia, and Vernon all contrast sharply with the more working-class name Harry. Dudley Dursley's name reflects the silliness of the character who bears it, not only in its stuttering quality ("Du-Du"), but also in the "dud" hidden in it. Dudley, we learn, is indeed a dud, and his name highlights the contrast between Harry's vitality and Dudley's absurdity. Furthermore, just as the Dursleys seem to be cartoonish versions of provincial English snobs, they are also cartoonish in their villainy. They are not just subtly bad toward Harry (as a real family might be) but outlandishly and unbelievably wicked in making him live in a cupboard under the stairs. Similarly, giving a boy thirty-seven birthday presents is not realistic, but in Rowling's fairy-tale world, we accept this exaggeration. The caricatured aspect of the characters thus helps us read the story as a myth.

Rowling exposes us to quite a bit of overt witchcraft in the first two chapters, such as Professor McGonagall's transformation into a cat. But Harry cannot identify magic when he sees it—even when it is his own magic, such as when he releases a boa constrictor at the zoo upon his enemies without being aware that he is doing it. He wonders how it happens and is mystified by it, but he never dreams it is magic. Harry's gradual understanding of this magic, proceeding from total ignorance to awareness to full mastery, is crucial to the story's development.

CHAPTER 3

SUMMARY

Punished for the boa constrictor incident, Harry is locked in his cupboard until summer. When finally free, he spends most of the time outside his house to escape the torments of Dudley's cohorts. Harry is excited by the prospect of starting a new school in the fall, far away from Dudley for the first time in his life. One day, Uncle Vernon tells Harry to fetch the mail. Harry notices a letter bearing a coat of arms that is addressed to him in "The Cupboard under the Stairs." Uncle Vernon grabs the envelope from him and shows it to his wife. Both are shocked. They force Dudley and Harry to leave the kitchen in order to discuss what to do. The next day, Uncle Vernon visits Harry in the cupboard. He refuses to discuss the letter, but he tells Harry to move into Dudley's second room, previously used to store Dudley's toys.

The next day, another letter comes for Harry, this time addressed to him in "The Smallest Bedroom." Uncle Vernon becomes alarmed. Harry tries to get the letter, but Uncle Vernon keeps it from him. The following morning, Harry wakes up early to try to get the mail before anyone gets up, but he is thwarted by Uncle Vernon, who has slept near the mail slot waiting for the letters. Though Uncle Vernon nails the mail slot shut, twelve letters come for Harry the next day, slipped under the door or through the cracks. Soon letters flood the house, entering in impossible ways. Uncle Vernon continues to prevent Harry from reading any of them. Enraged, Uncle Vernon decides to take everyone away from the house, but at the hotel where they stay, a hundred letters are delivered for Harry. Uncle Vernon decides on even greater isolation. On a dark, stormy night, he takes the family out to an island with only one shack on it. Inside, Vernon bolts the door. At midnight, as it becomes Harry's birthday, there is a loud thump at the door.

ANALYSIS

Harry's importance is becoming undeniable. While the disappearance of the snake tank's glass at the zoo might be passed off as a fluke, the letters that flood the Dursley home clearly point to some supernatural occurrence. While no one can be sure of Harry's role in the boa constrictor incident, the deluge of letters addressed to Harry shows indisputably that he has some link to magic. Though our sense of Harry's importance is growing, this importance remains unexplained. Rowling cleverly shows us the letters flooding in without initially letting us know what they say (the Dursley parents know, but we and Harry do not). It is far more effective that we do not know: whatever the letters say, the fact that so many of them arrive is reason enough to be awestruck, and they are more mysterious unopened.

Harry is simply impressed that the letters are addressed to him at all. Having lived in obscurity and neglect under the stairs, he has not been recognized as a person for ten years. Now the address to "Mr. H. Potter, The Cupboard under the Stairs" finally gives him a social identity. That they are addressed to "Mr. H. Potter," rather than simply to "Harry," reinforces the idea that Harry is gaining an adult identity.

The Dursleys' nighttime retreat to the deserted island heightens the suspense of the letters' significance. Rowling uses many of the elements of gothic literature, a genre of fiction that establishes an uneasy mood through the use of remote, desolate settings, supernatural or macabre events, and violence, to shroud this scene in an atmosphere of mystery and terror. The dark night, the terrible weather, and the desolate island build up the scene's tension until there is a climactic thump on the door at the stroke of midnight. With this thumping, we know that the Dursleys cannot possibly hide any longer from the supernatural forces at work.

CHAPTER 4

SUMMARY

But yeh must know about yer mom and dad. . . .
I mean, they're famous. You're famous.
(See QUOTATIONS, p. 52)

The thump is heard again. A giant smashes down the door. Uncle Vernon threatens the giant with a gun, but the giant takes the gun and ties it into a knot. The giant presents Harry with a chocolate birthday cake and introduces himself as Hagrid, the "Keeper of Keys and Grounds at Hogwarts." Hagrid is disturbed to find out that the Dursleys have never told Harry what Hogwarts is. Vernon tries to stop Hagrid from telling Harry about Hogwarts, but to no avail. Hagrid tells Harry that Harry is a wizard and presents him with a letter of acceptance to the Hogwarts School of Witchcraft and Wizardry. Vernon protests that he will not allow Harry to attend Hogwarts. Hagrid explains to Harry that the Dursleys have been lying all along about how the boy's parents died. Harry learns that they did not die in a car crash, as he had always thought, but were killed by the evil wizard Voldemort. Harry does not believe he could be a wizard, but then he realizes that the incident with the boa constrictor was an act of wizardry. With Uncle Vernon protesting, Hagrid takes Harry from the shack.

ANALYSIS

The arrival of Harry's birthday coincides with Hagrid's revelation of who Harry is, further suggesting that Harry must mature into his new identity. The time may be coming when Harry actually becomes a young Mr. H. Potter, as the letters refer to him, who lives his own life and is capable of making his own way. Even the chocolate cake that Hagrid brings for his birthday shows that, for the first time, Harry is no longer dependent on the Dursleys to feed him. His departure from home at the end of Chapter 4 is symbolic of this maturation. Harry can begin to imagine a future life of adult self-reliance, and we see that the story is perhaps a tale about growing up.

The dramatic conflict in the shack between Mr. Dursley and Hagrid sharply illustrates the contrast between the world of wizards and the world of ordinary Muggles. These two worlds are each represented by authority figures, and we see how Mr. Dursley's frantic obstinacy is very different from Hagrid's confident power. Mr. Dursley clings to his dominant role in the family with a pathetic desperation, but we see that Harry, like any boy in his right mind, prefers to associate with the dynamic and direct Hagrid. The flimsy social world represented by the Dursley family is crashing down, and we see a more appealing world of power and charisma emerging as an alternative. This opposition between Mr. Dursley and Hagrid can hardly be called a power struggle, as Hagrid is so easily the victor in the standoff between the two men. When he effortlessly bends Dursley's gun, we see that there can be no real contest between them. What is also interesting about the opposition between Muggles and wizards is that the Dursleys are aware of the two worlds the whole time. Rowling could have made the Dursleys oblivious of wizardry until Hagrid's arrival; instead, she has them live in denial for ten years. Their denial is intriguing because it suggests that normal people repress difficult or potentially embarrassing facts in order to make their lives seem more normal.

CHAPTERS 5–6

SUMMARY: CHAPTER 5

Harry wakes up in the company of Hagrid and realizes that the preceding night was not a dream. The two set off to London to shop for Harry's school supplies. Harry is concerned about the money required, but Hagrid assures him that his parents left behind plenty of funds for him at Gringotts, the wizards' bank run by goblins. Their first stop in London is at the Leaky Cauldron, a pub where all the patrons recognize Harry and are both nervous and honored to have the opportunity to meet him. They head out to the street, where Hagrid taps on a brick wall, and a small street called Diagon Alley opens before them. Hagrid explains that Harry will buy what he needs for school here. They go to Gringotts, where they are escorted down to Harry's safe. Inside, they view the piles of silver and gold that Harry's parents left him. Hagrid explains the complex wizard monetary system, which is composed of Galleons, Sickles, and Knuts. Hagrid fills a small bag with money. He then takes Harry to another vault, number 713, which is empty except for a grubby little package that Hagrid picks up and hides in his clothes, warning Harry not to ask about it.

Hagrid then takes Harry to be fitted for his uniform. In the store, he encounters a snobbish and unlikable boy who will also be starting Hogwarts in the fall. The snobbish boy talks highly about grand old wizard families, and Harry begins to worry about whether he is cut out to be a wizard. But Hagrid reassures Harry, telling him that he will learn all he needs to know and that there are many Muggle students at Hogwarts. After buying the required books and ingredients for potions, Hagrid and Harry then head to the wand store. Mr. Ollivander, the storeowner, makes Harry try a number of magic wands, telling him that it will be clear when he has the right one. Harry tries out many wands. Finally, he picks up one made of holly and phoenix feather, and sparks shoot out from it—this is clearly the right wand. Ollivander tells Harry that the only other wand containing feathers from the same phoenix belonged to Voldemort and had been used to give Harry his lightning-bolt forehead scar.

SUMMARY: CHAPTER 6

Harry's last month with the Dursleys is unpleasant. The day before he is due to leave, Harry asks Uncle Vernon to take him to the train station. Uncle Vernon agrees to take him but ridicules him for saying he is to leave from track nine and three quarters, as is marked on the ticket Hagrid gave him. The following day, Harry arrives at the station and stands between tracks nine and ten, wondering with increasing alarm how to find track nine and three quarters. Finally, he overhears some people mention Hogwarts; it is a family of red-haired children who seem to be bound for the academy. He asks the mother for help, and she tells him to walk through the barrier between tracks nine and ten. Harry does so, and he is astonished to find the train to Hogwarts on the other side. Harry boards it.

On the train, Harry is introduced to Fred and George Weasley, twins who are returning to school, and to their brother Ron, another student who will be starting at Hogwarts. Ron introduces Harry to such details of wizard life as Quidditch (a game a bit like soccer, but played on broomsticks), Famous Witches and Wizards cards (collectible items like baseball cards), and Every Flavor Beans. One of the cards bears the picture of Albus Dumbledore. Ron, who comes from a poor family, cannot afford the pastries sold on the train, so Harry buys a lot with his newfound wealth and shares them with Ron. Harry also meets a somewhat annoying, overachieving girl named Hermione Granger and sees again the unpleasant boy from the uniform shop, whose name is Draco Malfoy. All the students have heard of Harry, and Harry is not sure how to respond to his fame. Arriving at the station, the newcomers are led onto boats in which they sail to the castle of Hogwarts.

SUMMARY & ANALYSIS

ANALYSIS: CHAPTERS 5–6

The shopping trip to Diagon Alley and the train journey to Hogwarts represent not a total abandonment of Harry's earlier life, but in many ways represents a more magical and mythical version of it. The Muggles' world and the wizards' world are not opposites, but parallels. Certainly there are major differences as far as Harry is concerned; whereas in the Muggle world he is dependent on the Dursleys and is relegated to cramped living spaces, he now has money and respect. But the two worlds themselves are not so very different. For instance, there is snobbery and condescension in both. Harry has not escaped the selfish Dudley entirely, because Dudley is in a sense reborn in the figure of Draco Malfoy, another snob who revels in making Harry feel socially inferior. Draco, like Dudley, considers himself superior to Harry because he belongs to an established family while Harry is an outsider. Moreover, just as the name Dudley Dursley contrasts with the name Harry Potter, so does the name Draco Malfoy. Draco was the name of a harsh ancient Greek lawmaker and is also the Latin word for "dragon"; Malfoy is an Anglicized version of the French words mal and foi, which mean, roughly, "bad faith." Draco Malfoy can thus be seen as a more villainous (and more glamorous) version of Dudley Dursley.

Similarly, money drives both worlds. The wizard realm is not a money-free paradise, but is like a mirror of the Dursleys' consumerist world, complete with banks, shops, and candy vendors. Nothing in Diagon Alley is handed out for free; everything must be bought and paid for with an alternate currency, but the coins are minted in gold and silver just as in the Muggle world. There is outright wickedness in both the Muggle world and the wizard world. The villainous Voldemort matches the cruelly neglectful Dursleys in evil. All this shows that Harry's exciting new life will not be simply a withdrawal from his earlier misery into some cushy new heaven. His new life will not necessarily be safer or easier than the old one. What is different is not the world so much as Harry's role in it; his powers and status have increased enormously. He has been reborn—like the phoenix that gives his wand its powers—into much the same world as before, but with a new and different life.

Harry's acquisition of his magic wand is a key symbol of his new identity. It symbolizes his fate, as he does not choose the wand he wants, but is chosen by it, just as he is chosen by fate to be a wizard. His own will and preference do not matter; his wizardry is beyond personal choice. The wand also connects Harry to his past and to his future. The storeowner remembers clearly the wands he once sold to Harry's mother and father, which were made of willow and mahogany, respectively. These details give Harry a more concrete view of his parents than he has ever had (foreshadowing the family photos that Hagrid later gives Harry). Furthermore, because Harry's wand is similar to the wand that Voldemort used to give Harry his lightning-bolt scar, this wand directly connects him to the trauma of losing his parents, a loss that changed his life. Yet the future is suggested as much as the past; it is clearly foreshadowed that the wand and the wand's twin, which is in Voldemort's possession, will be used in a final, climactic standoff between good and evil. Finally, the wand is a symbol of Harry's new hero status—it is as though Harry is to redeem the world's goodness. As Voldemort's ultimate rival, Harry is set up as Voldemort's potential equal. This hero status is evident on the shopping trip and on the train, where Harry's new acquaintances are all aware of his fame. The magic wand, still unused but potentially powerful, is a fitting emblem of Harry's immense and untapped skill.

CHAPTERS 7–8

SUMMARY: CHAPTER 7

> *[T]here was a burst of green light and Harry woke, sweating.*
>
> (See QUOTATIONS, p. 53)

The new students are greeted at the castle door by Professor McGonagall, who tells them they will soon be sorted into their houses. All Hogwarts students live in one of four residences: Gryffindor, Hufflepuff, Ravenclaw, or Slytherin. Each house has its own team for Quidditch, a game that resembles soccer on broomsticks. The houses are in a yearlong competition with one another to acquire the most points, which are earned by success in Quidditch games and lost for student infractions. As the students enter Hogwarts, ghosts appear in the hallway. The students are led to the Great Hall, where the entire school waits for them. They see a pointy hat on a stool. When the students try on the hat, it announces the house in which they are placed. Harry becomes very nervous. He has learned that he does not care for Slytherin house, as the students in it are unpleasant and Voldemort once belonged to Slytherin. Finally, it is Harry's turn to wear the hat. After a brief mental discussion with the hat in which it tries to suggest Slytherin to him, the hat places Harry in Gryffindor. Harry is pleased to find that he is joined in Gryffindor by Ron and Hermione. Draco Malfoy is placed in Slytherin.

Everyone sits down to a grand feast to begin the year. Harry is overwhelmed by the variety of luscious food served. Sir Nicolas de Mimsy-Porpington, the resident ghost of Gryffindor (popularly known as Nearly Headless Nick because of a botched decapitation), introduces himself to the first-year students and tells them he hopes they will win the house championship this year. Over dessert, the discussion turns to the children's upbringings. A student named

Neville tells how his family thought he was a Muggle until he survived a fall from a window. Harry glances around the room and notices a few of the teachers talking to one another. One of them stares malevolently at Harry, who immediately feels a sharp pain in his forehead scar. Harry finds out that this man is Professor Snape, who teaches Potions. After dessert, Albus Dumbledore, the head of Hogwarts, gets up to make his welcome speech. He adds a few warnings about staying away from the Forbidden Forest and avoiding the third-floor corridor on the right side of the school. Everyone sings the school song and goes off to his or her house.

SUMMARY: CHAPTER 8

Harry finds life at Hogwarts unfamiliar and strange. Everyone talks about him, and an adult always seems to be around when he is doing something wrong. Harry finds all the classes interesting, with the exception of the History of Magic. In the first Transfiguration class (where students are taught how to turn one thing into another), only Hermione is able to make any progress at turning a match into a needle. Harry is relieved to see that others are just as lost as he is.

During breakfast the first Friday, Harry's owl, Hedwig, who delivers mail, arrives with a tea invitation from Hagrid. Later, in his Potions class, Harry discovers that Professor Snape really does not like him, mocking Harry as "our new celebrity" and then humiliating Harry for his ignorance of herbs. Harry brings Ron with him to Hagrid's shack for tea. Harry and Ron are disconcerted by Hagrid's huge and fierce-looking dog, Fang, but discover that he is gentle. Hagrid tells Harry that he is overreacting to Snape's treatment, asserting that Snape would have no reason to hate him. Harry happens to notice an article from the wizard newspaper detailing a break-in that occurred at Gringotts bank in a vault that had been emptied earlier in the day. He realizes that it happened on his birthday, the day he and Hagrid went to Gringotts. Furthermore, he remembers that Hagrid emptied vault seven hundred and thirteen, taking a small package with him as he left. Harry leaves Hagrid's, his mind filled with questions.

ANALYSIS: CHAPTERS 7–8

Harry's experience with the Sorting Hat is an important event in his development at Hogwarts. He dreads putting it on because he fears that the hat will assign him to Slytherin, which he associates with unlikable students. He assumes that the hat has all the power and that the student has no say in his or her own future. But when he puts the hat on, it actually seems to negotiate with Harry, tempting him with Slytherin but willing to accept Harry's refusal. This interaction is significant, as it shows that while much of Harry's fate has been decided for him (like his being a wizard), he still has some control over what he makes of his life. The hat says that Harry could be great in Slytherin rather than make a prophecy that he will be great, as if to emphasize that Harry is free to actualize or not to actualize his potential, as he wishes. In letting Harry choose between the dark and suspect Slytherin and the friendlier and nobler Gryffindor, the hat is allowing Harry to choose as well between goodness and wickedness. We feel that while Harry's fate may have been handed to him, what he does with that fate in his life will be his own achievement and will reflect his own character.

The hat also gives Harry his first real compliment in the story, telling him that he has "plenty of courage. . . [n]ot a bad mind. . . talent. . . and a nice thirst to prove yourself." What is important here is not just the hat's positive judgment of Harry, but the fact that Harry hears this positive opinion directly. Even though Harry is famous throughout the wizards' world, his Muggle family has raised him to think little of himself. All the rumors circulating about Harry's talents have not yet been verified, so it is hard for Harry to have a clear idea of his abilities. The hat, with its unquestioned authority, gives Harry the first real vote of confidence in which he can fully believe. It also gives him his first hint that he will need to use his powers. The hat's reference to Harry proving himself hints at his coming struggle with his enemies, foreshadowed by the dark look that Professor Snape gives him and the news about the attempted robbery of vault seven hundred and thirteen.

Family origins continue to be important in these chapters. During dessert at the welcome banquet, Harry's new classmates discuss their pasts, and Harry is told that some of the students are not from wizard families. The father of a boy named Seamus is a Muggle, and for a long while Neville's parents thought Neville was a Muggle. Hermione comes from a purely Muggle family. Yet these variations are of no importance at Hogwarts, which is an equal-opportunity wizards academy. The students of mixed or Muggle backgrounds are accepted on equal footing with the more illustrious wizards' offspring like Draco Malfoy. Indeed, having magic in the family is no guarantee of being exceptional or even rich. Ron Weasley, Harry's first friend at Hogwarts, is the child of a family with a very strong magic tradition, but Ron cannot even afford snacks on the train ride to school. Learning that family origins are not as important as talent and hard work at Hogwarts allows Harry to break away once and for all from the snobbish class-dominated world of the Dursleys.

Rowling continues to show that while Harry has great potential, he is ordinary in some ways. He is not an expert wizard; rather, like his peers who are just starting out at Hogwarts, he must learn how to use magic. And like any student, he sometimes has trouble in his classes, does not like all of his teachers, and gets annoyed by students who know how to do everything perfectly. The fact that he is flawed makes it easier for us to relate to him.

CHAPTER 9

SUMMARY

Harry is upset by news that the Gryffindors will have flying lessons with the Slytherins, because he does not want to spend more time with his Slytherin enemy Draco Malfoy. Madam Hooch leads the class, gently sending the new fliers off the ground. Neville has an accident and breaks his wrist. Madam Hooch takes him to the hospital, telling everyone to stay on the ground while she is away. Malfoy notices a magic ball belonging to Neville, picks it up, and begins to fly around with it. Harry goes after Malfoy, who throws the ball in the air. Harry catches it spectacularly and lands safely back on ground. Just then, Professor McGonagall arrives, reprimanding Harry and ordering him to follow her. But instead of punishing him, McGonagall introduces him to Oliver Wood, captain of the Gryffindor Quidditch team, explaining that Harry will make an excellent Quidditch player.

At dinner, Harry excitedly tells Ron about joining the Quidditch team but tells him that Wood wants it to be a secret. Malfoy comes over with his cronies Crabbe and Goyle and teases Harry about getting in trouble earlier. The tension grows and Malfoy challenges Harry to a wizard's duel. Harry accepts, in spite of Hermione's attempt to dissuade them from breaking the school rules. As Harry and Ron sneak out later that night, Hermione tries to stop them but gets locked out of the dorm and must tag along. Neville, wandering around lost, also joins them. They arrive at the trophy room, the site of the duel, but Malfoy is nowhere to be found. Suddenly, they hear

Argus Filch, the school caretaker, and his cat, Mrs. Norris, enter the room. They begin to hide and then run away. Not sure where they are going, they accidentally end up in the forbidden area on the third floor, staring at a large and scary three-headed dog. The children manage to get back to their dorm safely, though they are terrified. Hermione reprimands Harry but stirs his curiosity by pointing out that the dog was standing on a trapdoor.

ANALYSIS

Harry's chance discovery of the forbidden hallway on the third floor is important in several ways. It reminds us that there is more happening at Hogwarts than simply education and that the classroom is only one part of his experience at the academy. Furthermore, the hallway discovery serves as Harry's entry into the snooping and sleuthing role that he maintains throughout the rest of the story. When Hermione tells him that the dog was standing on a trapdoor, Harry realizes that whatever Hagrid took from vault seven hundred and thirteen is being guarded by the dog at Hogwarts. It is significant that Harry's first discovery of an important clue in the mystery at the heart of the story involves a transgression of a school rule. Dumbledore clearly spells out in his welcome speech that the hallway is forbidden, yet this hallway is precisely where Harry ends up. Harry's willingness to commit misdemeanors even at the start of his Hogwarts career makes him a more complex character. We feel with certainty that he is not bad, but we see that he has the healthy curiosity of any child in a new, exotic, and fascinating place.

We see that Harry's rebellious disregard for the rules may lead to some important knowledge, echoing an idea in the biblical story of Adam and Eve's fall in Eden: seeking forbidden knowledge may be punishable, but it is also what makes us human. The same association between breaking the rules and transcending one's position is noticeable in Harry's flying-lesson escapade. Harry clearly flouts the law by flying into the air after Neville's stolen ball, but his act is noble and displays his flying talents. Professor McGonagall may go through the motions of punishing Harry for breaking the rule, but her true feelings are praise and admiration. The idea that a little rule-breaking may be acceptable and even valued is one of the most interesting aspects of the novel's moral dimension.

SUMMARY & ANALYSIS

CHAPTER 10

SUMMARY

The next morning, Harry and Ron are discussing what the dog could be guarding when the mail arrives. Harry receives a first-class broomstick, along with a note from Professor McGonagall summoning him to Quidditch practice. Malfoy tells Harry that first-year students are not allowed broomsticks. When he tries to report Harry to Professor Flitwick, Flitwick just expresses admiration for Harry's talent. Harry later meets Oliver Wood to learn the basics of Quidditch. On Halloween, Flitwick begins teaching his students how to make things fly. Only Hermione succeeds; Ron, offended by her air of superiority, makes a nasty comment that Hermione overhears. Harry notices her running off in tears.

Harry and Ron arrive at the Halloween feast to hear Professor Quirrell, the teacher of Defense against the Dark Arts, give a terrifying announcement about a twelve-foot troll in the building. As the prefects lead the students back to their dorms, Harry realizes that Hermione does not know about the troll. They head off to warn her and come upon the troll. Unwittingly, they lock it in the girls' bathroom only to realize that Hermione is trapped in there with the troll. Using teamwork and magic, the three of them manage to knock out the troll. Professor McGonagall finds them and begins to scold the boys. Hermione interjects that Harry and Ron were looking for her. She then lies, saying that she went to face the troll herself and that Ron and Harry had been trying to save her from it. At this point, Hermione becomes their friend.

ANALYSIS

The troll episode sheds light on the institution of Hogwarts, as well as on various characters in it. It is surprising to see the general alarm created by the sighting of a troll within the castle walls, where so many bizarre and somewhat frightening creatures reside. Professor Quirrell is even more flustered than usual by the sight of the monster, and the students are rushed off to the safety of their dormitories. We see that despite the Hogwarts professors' great mastery of magic, they are far from invincible, being frightened by a troll of striking stupidity. We may wonder why one of the wizards does not simply put a spell on the castle to prevent trolls from entering or immobilize the intruding troll with a charm. Yet they do not, thus displaying the limits of their magic. Aa Harry is in a position to be awed by the majesty of Hogwarts, this timely show of the Hogwarts staff's vulnerability is a reminder to him that even the eminent academy may need his help—as he indeed discovers soon enough.

Harry's victory over the troll is his first true achievement at school, and its symbolic importance is considerable. Furthermore, the troll incident casts a suspicious light on Professor Snape, whom Harry notices sneaking off toward the third floor. Especially in light of Harry's belief that Snape hates him, Snape's sneaking away reinforces Harry's growing belief that Snape is evil. Finally, Hermione's character develops in the troll scene. For the first time, she breaks out of her overeager, goody-two-shoes role and lies to a teacher. By dropping her perfectionist facade, she appears more human to Harry and Ron. Her willingness to lie to protect her classmates makes her a much more likable and sympathetic individual, which enables Ron and Harry to become friends with her.

CHAPTER 11

SUMMARY

The Quidditch season begins, and Harry is about to play in his first match against Slytherin. To prepare, Harry borrows a book entitled *Quidditch Through the Ages* from Hermione. Professor Snape discovers Ron, Harry, and Hermione out with the book one evening and confiscates it from Harry on the feeble pretext that library books may not be taken outside. Harry's suspicions of Snape continue to grow. Harry notices that Snape is limping. Going off to retrieve the book from Snape, Harry overhears Snape talking to Argus Filch about the three-headed dog, which makes Harry even more suspicious.

The next morning, the Quidditch match begins. Harry plays the position of Seeker, which means he must capture a little object called the Golden Snitch. He spots it and is flying toward it when the Slytherin Seeker pushes him out of the way and is penalized. Later in the game, Harry's broom begins moving uncontrollably. Hagrid comments that only dark magic could make a broomstick so hard to manage. Hermione notices that Snape is staring at Harry and muttering to himself. As the Weasley twins try to rescue their teammate Harry, Hermione rushes over to Snape, sneaks behind him, and sets his robe on fire. Suddenly, the spell on Harry's broom is broken and Harry is once again in control. He starts speeding toward the ground and lands, catching the Snitch.

Hagrid takes Harry back to his hut with Hermione and Ron, who tells Harry that Snape was putting a curse on his broomstick. Hagrid does not believe this charge, asking why Snape would try to kill Harry. Harry tells Hagrid about Snape getting injured by the dog in the third-floor corridor. Hagrid involuntarily reveals that the three-headed dog, Fluffy, is his, and that what the dog is guarding is a secret known only to Albus Dumbledore and a man named Nicolas Flamel.

ANALYSIS

The good and the wicked sides of Hogwarts become more distinct in these chapters as the novel's major characters begin to move into opposition. Just as the Quidditch players are divided into two opposing teams, Hogwarts separates into those allied with Dumbledore's rightful authority and those, like Snape, who seem to be plotting some wrongdoing against it. Harry's success at Quidditch foreshadows his later successful role in the more important standoff between good and bad in the story, and so it is significant that such an outright sign of evil occurs during the Quidditch game. We see that identifying one's enemy is a key part of any game strategy, and when Hermione notices that Snape seems to be muttering a curse on Harry's broomstick, it is suggested that teamwork is equally necessary. Hermione is playing on Harry's team just as much as his Quidditch teammates are, only in a different and more important game. Her role is just as important as Harry's, because without her assistance Harry might have fallen from his broomstick to his death. Though it is merely a game, Quidditch is given such significance throughout the story precisely because it demands both individual talent and teamwork in equal measure. Harry's education at Hogwarts teaches him not just that he has unique magic powers, but also that he needs to cultivate friends and allies if he is going to be able to use these powers effectively.

The game takes on greater significance, however, with the idea that it is not merely a contest between noble Gryffindors and cunning Slytherins but between good and evil. Hagrid's comment that only dark magic could make Harry's broomstick wobble so much indicates that the game has evolved from being a relatively friendly competition to being one of outright hostility. The use of dark magic forces Harry to face a more urgent threat—the need to survive. Hermione's decision to help save Harry's life by setting fire to Snape's robe demonstrates how the game's heightened stakes result in heightened motivations and consequences. As the forces of good and evil in the story draw closer, these motivations and consequences continue to intensify.

CHAPTERS 12–13

SUMMARY: CHAPTER 12

> *Your father left this. . . before he died. It is time it was returned to you.*
>
> (See QUOTATIONS, p. 54)

Christmas is approaching. Malfoy teases Harry about having to stay at Hogwarts for the holiday as he does not have parents. Harry, however, is looking forward to spending Christmas away from the Dursleys, especially because Ron is also staying at Hogwarts. The day before vacation, Hermione tears Ron and Harry away from a conversation with Hagrid to look in the library for more information about Nicolas Flamel. The librarian catches Harry prowling around the restricted-books section of the library and kicks him out.

On Christmas day, Harry and Ron awaken to presents, though Harry's are fewer. Harry receives candy and a knitted sweater from Ron's mother. He also receives an invisibility cloak accompanied only by an anonymous note telling him that the cloak once belonged to Harry's father. That night, after a satisfying Christmas dinner and after Ron has fallen asleep, Harry tries on his invisibility cloak. Unseen, he is able to go to the library's restricted-books section. But one of the books starts screaming when he opens it, so he quickly leaves. He passes Filch and hides in an old classroom marked with an inscription that includes the word "Erised." Inside stands an old mirror. Harry looks in the mirror and sees many people standing behind him, but when he turns around in the room, he sees no one. Suddenly, he recognizes that two of the people in the mirror are his dead mother and father. He tries to speak to them, but they can only communicate by waving. Harry lingers there a while but eventually returns to his room.

The next night, Harry brings Ron with him to the mirror room. Ron does not see Harry's parents in the mirror, but instead sees himself holding a Quidditch cup. Mrs. Norris, Filch's prowling cat, notices them. On the third night, Ron is afraid of being caught and does not want to go back, so Harry returns alone. There he finds Albus Dumbledore. Dumbledore explains to Harry that the mirror displays the deepest desire of whoever looks into it. Harry is relieved to find that Dumbledore is not angry.

SUMMARY: CHAPTER 13

Harry heeds Dumbledore's advice to stop visiting the Mirror of Erised. After Christmas break, Harry, Ron, and Hermione resume their search for Nicolas Flamel, though Harry's time is increasingly consumed by Quidditch practice. At practice one day, Harry learns that Snape will be refereeing the next game. He and his friends wonder whether Snape might try to harm Harry during the game. As they are talking, Neville hops by; Malfoy has cast a spell on him that has locked his legs together. Harry tells Neville that Neville needs to learn to stand up to Malfoy. Neville turns to leave, but not before giving Harry a Famous Wizard card for his collection. Suddenly Harry remembers where he has seen the name Nicolas Flamel before—on the back of the Albus Dumbledore Famous Wizard card that Ron gave him on the train trip to Hogwarts. Hermione runs to her room to get a book informing them that Flamel, once Dumbledore's partner, was the only wizard ever to make a Sorcerer's Stone. They learn that the Sorcerer's Stone transforms any metal into gold and produces an elixir of everlasting life. Harry and his friends conclude that the fierce dog on the third floor must be guarding Flamel's stone.

Harry's nervousness grows as the big Quidditch match approaches. If Gryffindor wins, it will take first place in the house championship. But Harry is concerned about Snape's evil plans. His fears are allayed when he learns that Dumbledore will be at the game, because Snape would never commit any wrongdoing in front of Dumbledore. In the game, Harry catches the Golden Snitch within the first five minutes, and the crowd roars. Dumbledore congratulates Harry for this astonishing feat. Afterward, Harry notices Snape heading off into the forest. He flies to follow him and hears Snape talking harshly in the forest to Professor Quirrell and mentioning the Sorcerer's Stone.

ANALYSIS: CHAPTERS 12–13

Harry's discovery of the Mirror of Erised is important both as plot development and as a revelation of Harry's own character. The mirror room is a taboo zone, and thus once again, Harry's entry is another violation of the rules. Harry finds the mirror in a room where he is not supposed to be, having just fled from the restricted-books section of the library where he is also not supposed to be. But it is a crucial scene, as it is the room in which the climactic encounter of the story later takes place. It is also the site of the first intimate and friendly conversation between Harry and Dumbledore, foreshadowing Harry's future successes in fighting for Dumbledore's side in the coming clash. Symbolically, the Mirror of Erised is a mirror into the soul, because it depicts the heart's deepest desire ("Erised" is "desire" spelled backward). Harry finds out nothing about the mysterious Nicolas Flamel, but he finds out a lot about his love for his long-dead parents and his wish that they were alive again. Like the invisibility cloak that also appears in this chapter, the Mirror of Erised helps Harry connect his present adventures with the past world of his parents and the fond feelings that dwell in his heart. As it turns out, this understanding of desire is much more important for Harry than the information that any book could convey. The turn from the outer world of library research to the inner world of memories and desires suggests that part of Harry's search involves an inward investigation of his own self.

Harry's growing intimacy with Dumbledore is an important development. At the beginning, Dumbledore is a rather abstractly presented grand person whom we glimpse from afar when he gives the students a welcome speech the night of their arrival. But when Dumbledore comes upon Harry in the mirror room, the old wizard and the young boy are alone for the first time in the story, conversing privately, and we see a more human side of Dumbledore. There is an increasing sense that Dumbledore cares about Harry as an individual, as there is no mention of him having a private audience with any other Hogwarts student. Even more important, Dumbledore surprises Harry at a very intimate moment of self-exploration, when Harry is examining his soul's deepest desires. Dumbledore's explanation of the mirror and gentle advice that Harry not consult it anymore show that the great wizard is a wise psychologist, as well as almost a father figure for Harry.

Dumbledore continues to be a protective force for Harry. His advice to refrain from looking in the Mirror of Erised stems from his understanding that the mirror's powerful images might overwhelm the young Harry. In contrast to Snape, who mocks Harry's celebrity status without hesitation, Dumbledore understands that Harry is a still a little boy with emotional needs. The later revelation that Dumbledore is the one who gives Harry's father's invisibility cloak to Harry reinforces his fatherly role. Finally, with Harry's discovery that the secret of Nicolas Flamel's identity is actually in his own possession the whole time, in a collector's card in his pocket that depicts Dumbledore, we feel even more strongly that Dumbledore occupies a very personal and intimate place in Harry's life.

CHAPTER 14

SUMMARY

As Easter approaches, Hermione begins to worry about exams, while Harry and Ron merely try to keep up with the tremendous amount of homework assigned. One day, Hagrid comes upon them studying in the library. They bombard him with questions about the Sorcerer's Stone. He invites them to come and talk to him later but says he does not promise that he will reveal anything. They visit Hagrid's hut later, and Hagrid tells them he does not know what else is guarding the stone besides the three-headed dog. He does tell them which teachers cast spells to guard the stone. He adds that he will never give out any information on how to bypass the dog.

Hagrid shows the students a dragon egg that he won in a poker game the previous night. Dragons are illegal, but Hagrid wishes to raise one anyway. Later, Harry gets a note saying the dragon egg is hatching. Excitedly, he and his friends rush over to Hagrid's to watch the dragon's birth. The children realize that Hagrid must get rid of this dragon, which Hagrid names Norbert, before he grows too big. They decide to write to Charlie, Ron's older brother, who is studying dragons in Romania. Charlie agrees to help them and arranges for them to meet some of his friends to take the dragon away. The plan is set for the children to meet Charlie's friends at midnight one Saturday atop the tallest tower of the castle. They take the invisibility cloak and sneak up carrying Norbert. Charlie's friends come and take the dragon away. As they descend from the tower, they forget to wear the invisibility cloak, and Filch catches them.

ANALYSIS

Rowling fleshes out the character of Hagrid more fully in this chapter. Hagrid initially seems like an uncouth but affectionate and well-meaning oaf sincerely concerned for Harry's welfare after the boy's arrival at Hogwarts, sending him a much-appreciated invitation to tea. Hagrid's fondness for animals shows that he can see the gentle side of even fierce creatures, as he is the owner of the murderous three-headed dog he cutely names Fluffy. For Hagrid, even wild and monstrous nature is full of kindness; he simply cannot believe in the bad side of anything. Unfortunately, this naïveté makes him ill-equipped to understand the villainous plots afoot at Hogwarts, because he cannot imagine that anyone would want to unseat the beloved Dumbledore. This simple faith is not just wrongheaded but downright dangerous, because, as we later discover, Hagrid's trust in a stranger who brings him a couple of drinks is what enables the villains to learn the secret of the guard dog.

Hagrid's optimism also keeps him from understanding the dangerous consequences of raising a dragon at home, not only because of the destructive potential of the beast, but also because it is a major offense and could get him and any accomplices into a lot of trouble. The dragon becomes a symbol of bad consequences that can come from good intentions. In insisting on seeing only the optimistic and kindly side of life, Hagrid makes us think about the dangers of being naïve and unaware of evil. In this sense, he makes us draw parallels between him and Harry, who may be similarly naïve. When Harry gets into trouble for helping Hagrid with his dragon, we see that being naïvely kind can be punished severely. Harry's awareness of evil is growing, as evidenced by the fact that he urges Neville to stick up for himself against the wicked Malfoy. But he still has some things to learn. Harry, like Hagrid, needs to think more critically and realistically about the consequences of his well-intended actions.

CHAPTER 15

SUMMARY

Filch takes Harry, Hermione, and Ron to Professor McGonagall's office to be punished. She accuses them of concocting the whole dragon story to lure Malfoy out of bed and get him into trouble. As punishment, McGonagall deducts fifty points from Gryffindor for each of the three wrongdoers. Harry is horrified that his house will lose 150 points. When the bad news is circulated the next morning, Harry quickly falls from his pedestal as Quidditch star. He considers resigning from the Quidditch team, but Wood convinces him that doing so would be useless.

Harry resolves not to get involved in any more suspicious activities, but a week later he overhears a conversation in which Quirrell appears to give in to someone, presumably Snape, as if Snape is pressing him to do something. Harry and his friends try to figure out what to do, but they cannot come up with a plan of action. Harry, Hermione, and Neville are told to report to Hagrid that night for their detention. When they show up, they are surprised to find that detention will be held in the surrounding Forbidden Forest. Malfoy, who has also been given detention, objects to being forced outside like a servant.

Hagrid points to some traces of unicorn blood on the ground and explains that they will be going into the forest to find out what has been harming the animals. They split up into two groups: Harry and Hermione with Hagrid, Neville and Malfoy with Hagrid's dog, Fang. They penetrate deep into the forest. Harry sees signs that the other group is in trouble, but Hagrid discovers that Malfoy has merely been playing tricks on Neville. Hagrid sends Harry off with Malfoy, taking Neville along with himself. Harry and Malfoy come across a mysterious cloaked figure drinking the blood of a recently killed unicorn. Malfoy and Fang run away, leaving Harry alone. A centaur named Firenze rescues Harry and carries him back to Hagrid. On his way back, Harry learns that the cloaked figure was Voldemort and that he was drinking unicorn blood to sustain himself until he could obtain the Sorcerer's Stone.

ANALYSIS

Death makes a sudden and violent appearance in these chapters. The spectacle of the dying unicorn that Harry glimpses in the forest is shocking not only because it is the first instance of death that we actually witness, but also because the unicorn is a symbol of innocence and purity. The murder of a unicorn, a harmless and delicate creature, displays death not as a natural process in the cycle of life, but as something wrongful and horrid. The death appears to be even more evil when we find out that the unicorn has died so that an evil being may live and that the wicked Voldemort drinks the unicorn's blood to sustain his own life while searching for immortality. Voldemort has flown in to steal something that does not belong to him, as his name reminds us: Vol de mort means either "flight of death" or "theft of death" in French. Both names suit the unjust death he brings.

The spectacle of Voldemort's exchange of death for life in the forest is important for Harry personally because he is the only one who witnesses it. We are reminded of another, much earlier moment of life and death in Harry's experience, also spent in the presence of Voldemort: the moment when Harry's life was saved in infancy while Voldemort killed Harry's parents. In medieval Europe, the unicorn was often a symbol of pure and selfless womanhood. Like Harry's mother, the unicorn dies protecting her baby son, perhaps even giving up her life so that her baby can live. Harry's investigation of the Hogwarts mystery is bringing him closer to his parents, unwittingly bringing their killer, Voldemort, to some sort of justice.

CHAPTER 16

SUMMARY

The year-end examinations go off without a hitch, although Harry fears that Voldemort will burst through the door at any second. While he is a guest at Hagrid's, Harry learns that while drunk and playing cards, Hagrid revealed to Voldemort that anyone can get past the three-headed guard dog, Fluffy, by playing music to him. Harry and his friends rush to find Dumbledore to tell him this news, but they run into McGonagall, who informs them that Dumbledore has been called off to London by the Ministry of Magic. Harry convinces Hermione and Ron that they need to grab the stone that night. As they are heading out, Neville tries to stop them. Hermione immobilizes him with a spell, and they proceed.

When they reach Fluffy, Harry, Hermione, and Ron notice a harp by his feet and realize that someone has already passed by Fluffy. Harry plays a flute he has brought, putting Fluffy to sleep and allowing his gang to go through the trapdoor. They land on some sort of plant with twisting tendrils that wrap around Harry and Ron. Hermione gets out immediately and uses fire from her wand to stave off the plant. Next, they encounter a large locked door in a room full of birds that are actually keys. Harry uses his Quidditch skills to catch the right bird and unlock the door. They then must play a violent game of chess in which each of them is a chess piece. Ron masterfully leads them through the game, but he must allow himself to be captured—and severely beaten—by the opposing queen to win. Harry and Hermione then come upon a series of potions and a logic puzzle. Hermione figures out which potions to drink and then goes back to help Ron and Harry move forward to find the stone.

ANALYSIS

Harry's breadth of wisdom is shown when he is forced to choose between obedience and fame on one hand and courage on the other and he opts for the latter. Hermione, who generally likes to follow rules, believes that Harry's plan to find the Sorcerer's Stone is crazy. Her fear that he will get expelled reflects her general concern about academic reputation. Harry, on the other hand, cares less about his status at school and more about the seemingly unavoidable battle between good and evil over the Sorcerer's Stone. In a memorably brave response to Hermione, Harry shouts, "SO WHAT? . . . If Snape gets ahold of the Stone, Voldemort's coming back! . . . There won't be any Hogwarts to get expelled from! . . . Losing points doesn't matter anymore." Harry is able to see beyond the limits of Hogwarts and glimpse the cosmic dimension of Voldemort's threats. He sees that the points system that dominates everyone's thinking in the school is trivial compared to the prospect that Voldemort will unleash evil upon the world. In this respect, Hermione's book-learning is contrasted with Harry's practical wisdom. Hermione receives a grade of 112 percent on her final exams and has read every textbook backward and forward, but she lacks Harry's key ability to view the broader consequences of facts. While Hermione has progressed a great deal, she fails to realize the full implications of the Sorcerer's Stone. Harry, by contrast, seems wise beyond his years, recognizing that at a certain point the glory and fame that come from being crowned house champions are less important than the battle between good and evil.

The obstacles that Harry, Hermione, and Ron encounter on their quest for the Sorcerer's Stone force each of them to use his or her individual talents and skills. Harry, for example, is an excellent broom-flyer, and his aerial agility enables him to grab the bird key that unlocks the door for them. Ron is a good chess player, and he willingly sacrifices his own body to win, allowing Harry and Hermione to advance. Hermione is an expert in logic, and she successfully picks out the right bottle for Harry so that he can advance toward the stone while she goes back to help Ron. Rowling thus emphasizes the importance of teamwork over individual accomplishment.

CHAPTER 17

SUMMARY

> *After all, to the well-organized mind, death is but the next great adventure.*
>
> (See QUOTATIONS, p. 55)

On the other side of the door, Harry is shocked to find Professor Quirrell, who explains that it was he, not Snape, who has been trying all along to kill Harry. Quirrell announces that he will kill Harry this night. In the room is the Mirror of Erised, which Quirrell says will help him finally find the stone. Harry, knowing that the mirror will show him what he most desires, realizes that what he wants most is to find the Sorcerer's Stone. Quirrell is engaged in a conversation with Voldemort, who speaks in a high voice from some hidden place. It turns out that Voldemort has been using Quirrell to get the stone for him. Voldemort tells Quirrell to use Harry to find the stone. Quirrell places Harry in front of the mirror and orders him to tell what he sees. Harry sees himself reaching into his pocket, pulling out a stone, and then dropping it back in his pocket. Simultaneously, he feels the actual stone in his pocket—as, we find out later, Dumbledore has wanted these things to happen all along.

Harry lies, telling Quirrell that he sees himself in the mirror winning the house cup for Gryffindor. Voldemort tells Quirrell that Harry is lying. Wishing to speak directly to Harry now, Voldemort tells Quirrell to unwrap his turban. Harry is shocked to find Voldemort's face on the back of Quirrell's head—Voldemort is a shapeshifter and has been using Quirrell's body. Voldemort tries to persuade Harry to give him the stone, which he knows is in Harry's pocket. He tells Harry to join him rather than resist and be killed like his parents. Harry refuses and Voldemort orders Quirrell to seize Harry. Quirrell tries, but each time he grabs for Harry, his hand blisters as if burned. Harry grabs Quirrell, putting him in tremendous pain; meanwhile, the pain in Harry's forehead scar is steadily increasing. As the struggle intensifies, Harry feels himself losing hold of Quirrell and falling.

When Harry regains consciousness, Dumbledore is standing over him. Harry starts telling Dumbledore that Quirrell has the stone, but Dumbledore tells him to relax. Harry realizes that he is in the hospital. He asks Dumbledore again about the stone and Dumbledore tells him that he arrived just in time to save Harry from Quirrell. Dumbledore adds that he spoke with Nicolas Flamel and they decided to destroy the stone. He explains also that Quirrell could not touch Harry because Harry was protected by his mother's love. Dumbledore also reveals that it was he who left the invisibility cloak for Harry and explains that there was enmity between Snape and Harry's father, much like the enmity between Malfoy and Harry. Furthermore, Dumbledore explains how Harry ended up with the stone; Harry was the only one who wanted to find the stone for itself rather than for what the stone could obtain.

Harry gets out of his hospital bed to go to the end-of-year feast. The dining hall is decorated in Slytherin colors to celebrate Slytherin's seventh consecutive win of the championship cup. Dumbledore rises to speak and announces that in light of recent events, more points need to be given out. He awards Ron and Hermione fifty points each and Harry sixty points for their feats in getting to the stone. Gryffindor thus pulls into a tie with Slytherin. Dumbledore then adds that Neville has been awarded ten points for learning bravery. Gryffindor pulls ahead into first place, thus winning the house cup.

When school grades finally arrive, Harry and Ron do well, and Hermione is at the top of the class. They all pack and head to the train station to go back to their homes. Harry, Hermione, and Ron say their good-byes for the summer and Harry heads home, eager to use a little magic on Dudley Dursley.

ANALYSIS

Quirrell's comment about the Sorcerer's Stone and his affections for Voldemort that "[t]here is no good and evil, there is only power and those too weak to see it" evoke important philosophical ideas. The sentiments Quirrell expresses underlie one of the classic works of political theory, Niccolò Machiavelli's *The Prince*. In this sixteenth-century work Machiavelli wrote about how rulers should expand their power with no regard for morality or justice. The distinction Quirrell makes here between "power" and "those too weak to see it" follows the principles that Machiavelli laid out. Quirrell's statement also echoes the thought of nineteenth-century

German philosopher Friedrich Nietzsche, who argued that individual human will and striving are more important and relevant than morality and more impressive than flimsy notions of right and wrong. The ideas of these two philosophers emphasize the individual at the expense of the common good, and Voldemort embodies their values.

By placing these sentiments in the mouth of Quirrell, who is as pathetic and squirrelly as his name suggests, Rowling rejects the idea that the world should be based on power and domination of others. It is fine to cultivate power; Dumbledore's power, after all, is exceptional and praiseworthy. But the story suggests that with power comes responsibility toward others and that responsibility includes a sense of what is right and wrong. Dumbledore shows the students that Slytherin House may have acquired a lot of points but that victory should go to the house that has been engaged in a just and righteous struggle. This is surely also the reason that Flamel is induced to destroy the Sorcerer's Stone; it is a source of incredible power, but there is no guarantee that its power will be used properly, and so it must be destroyed. Power is important, but morality is more so.

The wisdom of limiting one's desires is revealed at the end, when Dumbledore tells Harry that, for Nicolas Flamel, dying will be a pleasant experience of relief, "like going to bed after a very, very long day." Dumbledore's earlier advice to Harry to refrain from looking in the Mirror of Erised becomes relevant here, as Dumbledore suggests that while it is important to reflect on one's deepest desire, it is also important to keep that desire in perspective and perhaps even to limit it. Eternal life—the very thing promised by the Sorcerer's Stone and the very thing many have been desiring—might not be as valuable as those seeking it have thought. Flamel is close to achieving immortality, and yet he prefers to die. Dumbledore points out that living forever could actually become tiresome, and that the desire for it may be misinformed.

While Flamel and Dumbledore ultimately understand that eternal life may not be such a good goal, Voldemort's fatal flaw is that he is misinformed about what is important in life but is never able to realize it. Voldemort lives for his own desires, but as we discover toward the end, he is not really living at all: he does not even have his own body, but must live by stealing others' bodies (again, one meaning of the French word vol is "theft"). But Voldemort lacks more than a body; he lacks a soul as well. Living by desire, he has no real life. Nor does he have any love, as Dumbledore explains to Harry. Love is the one thing that Voldemort cannot understand, which is why he is burned by the traces of motherly love on Harry's body. The greatest lesson learned throughout this adventure may be that love for others is more valuable than the pursuit of one's own desires (which is really nothing more than love for oneself).

Important Quotations Explained

1. "My dear Professor. . . [a]ll this 'You-Know-Who'
    nonsense—for eleven years I have been trying to
    persuade people to call him by his proper name:
    Voldemort." Professor McGonagall flinched, but
    Dumbledore, who was unsticking two lemon drops,
    seemed not to notice.

Dumbledore's impatient reproach to Professor McGonagall occurs
in Chapter 1, when they and Hagrid appear in front of the Dursleys'
house to discuss the sudden tragic deaths of Harry's parents. The
passage reveals Dumbledore's composure even after a hugely trau-
matic event like an evil wizard's murder of two innocent people: he
is calmly using phrases like "My dear Professor" and eating candy,
while McGonagall is flinching with nervousness. We see clearly
why Dumbledore is head wizard and McGonagall his subordinate.

The passage also reveals the importance of facing one's enemies
directly. For all of McGonagall's education and expertise, she is
unable to speak Voldemort's name out loud, as are many other
Hogwarts residents. The implication is that they are too scared to
utter the name. Harry, we find out later, is, by contrast, not scared
at all; his friends keep urging him to say "You-Know-Who" instead
of "Voldemort," but he sees no reason to do so, and keeps forget-
ting. When Harry calls Voldemort by his proper name, we get a hint
that Harry will be the one who can face the evil wizard directly, as
he in fact does when he stares at Voldemort's face on the back of
Quirrell's head. Harry's directness is exactly what Dumbledore is
asking for from McGonagall and symbolizes the importance of con-
fronting one's obstacles.

2. "But yeh must know about yer mom and dad," he
    said. "I mean, they're famous. You're famous."

Hagrid says these words to Harry in Chapter 4, after bursting into
the hut on the secluded island where Mr. Dursley has brought Harry
to escape the magical letters. Hagrid's surprise at Harry's ignorance
of himself and of his family underscores the separation of the Muggle and the wizard worlds. Being famous among wizards does not
necessarily imply being famous among ordinary humans. Despite
all the vast powers of the wizards, the Hogwarts officials have been
unable to penetrate the defenses of stupid and selfish Muggles like
the Dursleys, who have, quite impressively, kept Harry's uniqueness a secret from him for ten whole years. The intense Muggle
dread of being different and the powerfully oppressive denials of
how Harry is special are actually quite a match for all the wizards at
Hogwarts. In Hagrid's astonishment that one could be a wizard
without realizing it, we see how stifling and constraining human
society can be, at least in the Dursley household.

   Hagrid's reference to Harry's parents in connection with Harry's
own fame foreshadows one important aspect of Harry's upcoming
adventures. His experiences at Hogwarts will prove how talented
Harry is ("You're famous"), but they will also re-establish the connection that has been lost between Harry and his real family. By
learning magic, Harry will earn the right to belong again in the company of his mother and father. Harry's education will take him not
just forward to his brilliant future, but also symbolically backward
to his original family.

QUOTATIONS

3.   He was wearing Professor Quirrell's turban, which
     kept. . . telling him he must transfer to Slytherin at
     once, because it was his destiny. . . . [H]e tried to pull
     it off but it tightened painfully—and there was
     Malfoy, laughing at him. . . . [T]here was a burst of
     green light and Harry woke, sweating.

Harry has this dream at the end of Chapter 7, and it reveals much
not only about Harry's fate and his situation, but also about Harry's
own challenge in having to deal with such a burden. Before describ-
ing this dream, the narrator suggests that the dream comes perhaps
because Harry has eaten too much, but we know better. We understand that Harry is wrestling with some very difficult issues that are
affecting his dreams. His dream of Quirrell is prophetic, as Harry
discovers only in Chapter 17 that Quirrell, not Snape, is behind the
evil plot; perhaps he suspected Quirrell unconsciously all along. The
talking turban clearly reminds us of the Sorting Hat, which represents fate for Harry in assigning him to a house at Hogwarts.

   The turban also reminds us how Voldemort talks to Harry much
later from under Quirrell's turban and how Voldemort and his evil
green light are also part of Harry's fate. But even fate is not so easy
to understand, as we recall that Harry is able to persuade the hat to
assign him to Gryffindor rather than Slytherin; perhaps fate can be
changed through personal actions, just as Harry tries to pull off the
turban of destiny in his dream. Finally, the presence of Malfoy in
Harry's dream shows that his adventure in solving the Sorcerer's
Stone mystery is intertwined with his more everyday task of having
social interactions, choosing friends, and facing down one's enemies. Malfoy plays no part in Voldemort's plot, but he seems important to Harry nevertheless, as one of the many confusing factors in
Harry's attempt to make sense of his Hogwarts experience.

QUOTATIONS

4. Your father left this in my possession before he died. It is time it was returned to you. Use it well. A very merry Christmas to you.

This note accompanies the vanishing cloak that Harry mysteriously receives at Christmas in Chapter 12. It signals once again that Harry's growth at Hogwarts will bring him back into contact, at least symbolically, with his long-lost parents. The cloak also becomes an important symbol of the relationship between Harry and Albus Dumbledore when we find out later that it is Dumbledore who has given the cloak to Harry. It symbolizes Dumbledore's growing trust in Harry, as the great wizard surely knows that giving a boy the gift of invisibility is bound to lead to some naughtiness, which it in fact does. Dumbledore may caution Harry to "[u]se it well," but in all his wisdom he must realize that Harry will use it wrongly, breaking into the restricted-books section of the library and hauling an illegal dragon across the campus.

Yet, in the long run, Dumbledore's trust in Harry is justified, because Harry does learn finally to use the cloak—and all his magic gifts—toward the right ends. His disaster in being caught and punished after the dragon incident, when he stupidly forgets to wear the cloak, forces him to think more carefully about the consequences of his actions. We sense that Harry's education in personal responsibility is all part of Dumbledore's grand plan in giving Harry the cloak, because after the dragon affair Dumbledore returns the cloak to Harry neatly folded. With it, Dumbledore places his own vote of confidence in Harry.

5.   After all, to the well-organized mind, death is but the
     next great adventure.

Dumbledore makes this remark to Harry in Chapter 17, when
Harry is in the hospital, in reference to the imminent death of
Nicolas Flamel, Dumbledore's old partner and inventor of the Sorcerer's Stone. When Dumbledore announces that he and Flamel
have decided to thwart Voldemort by destroying the stone, and
with it the possibility of attaining eternal life, Harry realizes that
Flamel will die. Flamel is effectively sacrificing himself for the good
of Hogwarts and of the world, just as Jesus Christ, according to
Christian belief, was supposed to have sacrificed himself for the
salvation of humankind. Flamel's decision reveals his wisdom, all
the more so as Dumbledore's words echo the thoughts of innumerable philosophers and religious figures (from the Greek Socrates to
the Indian Buddha) who have similarly seen death as a beginning
rather than an end.

   Dumbledore's and Flamel's wisdom is precisely what is lacking
in a villain like Voldemort, who clings unnaturally to life, refusing
to accept the natural human adventure of death. By saying that a
healthy acceptance of death is a characteristic of a "well-organized
mind," Dumbledore is implying that Voldemort's manic pursuit of
immortality is not well organized at all, despite all of his savvy
tricks, but is rather deranged.

QUOTATIONS

KEY FACTS

FULL TITLE
Harry Potter and the Sorcerer's Stone (originally titled *Harry Potter and the Philosopher's Stone*)

AUTHOR
J. K. Rowling

TYPE OF WORK
Novel

GENRE
Children's book, fantasy tale

LANGUAGE
English

TIME AND PLACE WRITTEN
1990s, Scotland

DATE OF FIRST PUBLICATION
1997

PUBLISHER
Bloomsbury Children's Books

NARRATOR
The story is narrated by a detached third-person observer close to the action, but not involved in it.

POINT OF VIEW
For most of the story, the narrator, who knows everything about all of the characters, generally stays close to Harry Potter's point of view, registering surprise when Harry is surprised and fear when Harry is afraid. But while Harry is a baby in the first chapter, the narrator takes the point of view of Mr. Dursley, who is perplexed by signs of wizards around town. The shift in point of view from a Muggle's perspective to a wizard's emphasizes the difference between the two worlds.

TONE
As fitting for a children's book, the tone is straightforward and simple, with few purely decorative elements or artistic features,

few metaphors and figures, and little playful irony. The language is easy to grasp. The narrator never imposes moral judgments on any characters, even the wicked Voldemort, but allows us full freedom to praise or condemn.

TENSE

Past

SETTING (TIME)

An unspecified time, modern and roughly contemporary (late 1990s)

SETTING (PLACE)

Surrey, England, and the Hogwarts wizardry academy

PROTAGONIST

Harry Potter

MAJOR CONFLICT

Harry attempts to stop Voldemort, who killed Harry's parents, from stealing the Sorcerer's Stone.

RISING ACTION

Harry's arrival at Hogwarts, the news of the break-in at Gringotts, and Hermione's revelation of the trapdoor under the guard dog in the third-floor corridor bring Harry and Voldemort closer to confrontation.

CLIMAX

Professor Snape's apparent hex on Harry during the Quidditch game brings the simmering tension between good and evil out into the open, shifting Harry's concern from winning the game to surviving.

FALLING ACTION

With the conflict out in the open, the forces of good and the forces of evil draw closer together: Harry, Ron, and Hermione explore the school and learn about the Sorcerer's Stone; Voldemort drinks unicorn blood to sustain himself and attacks Harry in the Forbidden Forest; Harry faces Professor Quirrell and Voldemort, who orders Quirrell to kill Harry.

THEMES

The value of humility, the occasional necessity of rebellion, the dangers of desire

MOTIFS

Muggles, points, authority

SYMBOLS

Harry's scar, Quidditch, the Mirror of Erised

FORESHADOWING

The pain that Harry feels at the end of Chapter 7 when Snape stares at him hints that there is some underlying tension between the two. Rowling exploits our misgivings about Snape by leading us to believe that he and Harry will eventually confront each other in a climactic battle for the Sorcerer's Stone.

KEY FACTS

STUDY QUESTIONS & ESSAY TOPICS

STUDY QUESTIONS

1. *Throughout most of the story, we share Harry's point of view. We see what he sees and experience what he experiences. In the first chapter, however, we are shown Mr. Dursley's point of view as he drives to work, sees a cat reading a map, and encounters oddly dressed people on the streets. Rowling could have given us a more straightforward third-person story without any particular point of view. Why does she choose to show us Mr. Dursley's thoughts and reactions in this first chapter?*

Rowling may start off with Mr. Dursley's narrow-minded and peevish point of view to help us distance ourselves from our Muggle way of thinking. In inviting us to make fun of Mr. Dursley's alarmed reaction to such harmless spectacles as men in green capes and cats with maps, Rowling allows us to feel different from Mr. Dursley and associate ourselves with a more interesting perspective and value system. No longer as deeply buried in the Muggle perspective as before, we are ready to be introduced to the wizards' world more fairly, through the more open-minded perspective of Harry. When we feel familiar with the world of Hogwarts, we can look back on Mr. Dursley's understanding of the wizards and realize how shallow and wrong he is. Wizards are not just eccentric caped figures with silly ways of speaking, but are agents of growth, wisdom, and self-discovery, as Harry and we find out over the course of the story.

2. *How does the Hogwarts world compare with the Muggle world? Does Rowling want us to make such a comparison?*

By setting up two parallel worlds that overlap in a few places (the wizard celebration in Chapter 1 has consequences in the Muggle world, for example), Rowling does indeed invite us to compare them. One of the striking things about such a comparison, however, is that the wizards' world and the Muggles' world are remarkably similar—perhaps even more similar than different. There is shopping on the magic Diagon Alley just as there is shopping in Muggle malls, and money must be used in both worlds to make purchases. Indeed, wealth matters in Hogwarts just as much as it does in the Dursleys' world. Also, there are snobs in Hogwarts: Malfoy is every bit as concerned with social prestige at Hogwarts as Mrs. Dursley is in the Muggle world. And friendship matters in both worlds: Dudley's friends are as important to him (though much more obnoxious) as Hermione and Ron eventually become to Harry at Hogwarts.

The real difference between the two worlds lies not in their appearances or social structures but in their attitudes toward human potential and human difference. While Hogwarts teaches students to develop their powers to the fullest extent possible, the Muggle world, as represented by the Dursleys, is intent on stifling uniqueness. Mrs. Dursley cares very much about public opinion and about what the neighbors are saying, and we see that being normal is far more important to her than being unusual, different, or special. This desire for normalcy no doubt explains why the Dursleys are so horrified by the prospect of Harry becoming a wizard. They dread his being different, just as they hated his mother's being different. The Hogwarts world provides Harry with what the Muggles forbid him: the chance to develop his true self.

3. *Harry has no personal contact with Dumbledore until he is caught in the forbidden room where the Mirror of Erised stands. Why does this first close contact with Dumbledore occur in the mirror room? Is the situation more important than just a routine rule violation by a naughty student? If so, how?*

The mirror room is the place where Dumbledore really makes an impression on Harry. Harry is impressed by the grandeur of the great wizard at the welcome ceremony, but he is not really personally touched. Harry's encounter with Dumbledore in the mirror room, however, is about something much more meaningful than a student's violation of a rule. Dumbledore is not present as a policeman but rather as a wise guide using the opportunity to help Harry learn about himself. In fact, Dumbledore does not even mention the fact that Harry has broken any rules; he just explains why it would be a good idea to avoid the mirror in the future.

Dumbledore begins to forge a more intimate relationship with Harry in the mirror room rather than elsewhere because the mirror is at the heart of the wisdom that he means to impart to Harry. Dumbledore does not care so much about the routine aspects—classes, exams, and rules—of Hogwarts so much as he cares that Harry adopt a proper attitude toward his own desires. He advises Harry to be modest in desire and not to forget that life is more important than dreams. Harry takes Dumbledore's message to heart, and we see that the aspect of wizardry most meaningful to Harry on a personal level is not the level of cloaks and spells but the deeper level of self-understanding.

QUESTIONS & ESSAYS

SUGGESTED ESSAY TOPICS

1. At the end of Harry's adventures, when the Sorcerer's Stone has been safely destroyed, Dumbledore reveals to Harry that he devised the Mirror of Erised in the knowledge that Harry would succeed where Voldemort would fail. This admission raises the question of whether Dumbledore orchestrates other parts of Harry's adventures too. Does he know, for instance, that the troll will be let into Hogwarts, and does he foresee Harry's defeat of the troll? Is it possible that Dumbledore has a godlike foreknowledge of the whole story from beginning to end?

2. When Harry chooses his wand on Diagon Alley, he finds that the one right for him is the companion wand to the one sold long ago to Voldemort. Why does Rowling choose to emphasize a curious affinity between Harry and his great enemy, Voldemort?

3. What does the episode of the Sorting Hat reveal about Harry? What does it say about fate in the story? Is it always superior to human will?

4. At the end of Chapter 7, Harry dreams of various suspicious Hogwarts figures involved in the mysterious plot he has uncovered, including Quirrell and Snape. Why, do you think, does Malfoy appear in the dream as well? Is Malfoy's role in the story deeper than it seems?

5. Why does the school first prohibit the Forbidden Forest and then force Harry to enter it for his detention? Has there been a change in opinion among the Hogwarts authorities as to Harry's ability to handle danger so that prohibitions are no longer as necessary as they used to be?

Review & Resources

Quiz

1. How does Harry first learn that he is a wizard?

    A. The Dursleys tell him when he is eight
    B. Dudley accidentally lets it slip
    C. Hagrid has to track him down to tell him
    D. He reads about it in the Daily Prophet

2. Where does Harry live in the Dursley's home?

    A. With Dudley
    B. In the guest house
    C. In Mr. and Mrs. Dursley's room
    D. In a cupboard under the stairs

3. Who decides where the children will be housed at Hogwarts?

    A. Albus Dumbledore
    B. The Sorting Hat
    C. The Sorting Broom
    D. Each child decides for him- or herself

4. How do the children get rid of Hagrid's dragon?

    A. They poison it
    B. They bring it up to the top of the tallest tower and push it off
    C. They bring it up to the top of the tallest tower and give it to Ron's older brother's friends
    D. They bring it up to the top of the tallest tower and give it to Voldemort

5.   What is significant about the day of the Gringotts break-in?

   A.   It occurs on Harry's birthday
   B.   Harry is at Gringotts earlier the same day
   C.   Hagrid empties vault seven hundred and thirteen
   D.   All of the above

6.   Who is Fluffy?

   A.   Hagrid's dragon
   B.   Harry's owl
   C.   Hagrid's three-headed dog
   D.   Dumbledore's pet snake

7.   Which teacher is trying to steal the Sorcerer's Stone?

   A.   Snape
   B.   Dumbledore
   C.   Quirrell
   D.   McGonagall

8.   To whom does the Sorcerer's Stone belong?

   A.   Harry
   B.   Hagrid
   C.   Voldemort
   D.   Nicolas Flamel

9.   What position does Harry play in Quidditch?

   A.   Quaffle
   B.   Sweeper
   C.   Seeker
   D.   Chaser

10.   What does Voldemort drink in the Forbidden Forest to sustain himself?

   A.   Apple nectar
   B.   Unicorn blood
   C.   Sacred water
   D.   Cedar sap

11. Whom do Harry and Ron accidentally lock in the bathroom with the troll?

    A.   Hermione
    B.   Dumbledore
    C.   Malfoy
    D.   McGonagall

12. What does Harry see when he looks in the Mirror of Erised for the first time?

    A.   Himself as an old, wise wizard
    B.   A Quidditch trophy
    C.   The Sorcerer's Stone
    D.   His parents

13. To whom does the invisibility cloak belong originally?

    A.   Harry's father
    B.   Voldemort
    C.   Dumbledore
    D.   Hagrid

14. In what house is Malfoy?

    A.   Hufflepuff
    B.   Slytherin
    C.   Gryffindor
    D.   Ravenclaw

15. Who actually puts the curse on Harry during the Quidditch match?

    A.   Snape
    B.   Malfoy
    C.   Quirrell
    D.   Nicolas Flamel

REVIEW & RESOURCES

ANSWER KEY:
1: C; 2: D; 3: B; 4: C; 5: D; 6: C; 7: C; 8: D; 9: C; 10: B; 11: A; 12: D; 13: A; 14: B; 15: C;

SUGGESTIONS FOR FURTHER READING

KRONZEK, ALLAN ZOLA AND ELIZABETH KRONZEK. *The Sorcerer's Companion: A Guide to the Magical World of Harry Potter.* New York: Broadway Books, 2001.

ROWLING, J. K. *Harry Potter and the Chamber of Secrets.* New York: Scholastic, Inc., 1999.

———. *Harry Potter and the Prisoner of Azkaban.* New York: Scholastic, Inc., 1999.

———. *Harry Potter and the Goblet of Fire.* New York: Scholastic, Inc., 2000.

———. *Fantastic Beasts and Where to Find Them.* New York: Scholastic, Inc., 2001.

———. *Quidditch Through the Ages.* New York: Scholastic, Inc., 2001.

REVIEW & RESOURCES

A Note on the Type

The typeface used in SparkNotes study guides is Sabon, created by master typographer Jan Tschichold in 1964. Tschichold revolutionized the field of graphic design twice: first with his use of asymmetrical layouts and sanserif type in the 1930s when he was affiliated with the Bauhaus, then by abandoning assymetry and calling for a return to the classic ideals of design. Sabon, his only extant typeface, is emblematic of his latter program: Tschichold's design is a recreation of the types made by Claude Garamond, the great French typographer of the Renaissance, and his contemporary Robert Granjon. Fittingly, it is named for Garamond's apprentice, Jacques Sabon.

SPARKNOTES
TEST PREPARATION
GUIDES

The SparkNotes team figured it was time to cut standardized tests down to size. We've studied the tests for you, so that SparkNotes test prep guides are:

Smarter:
Packed with critical-thinking skills and test-
taking strategies that will improve your score.

Better:
Fully up to date, covering all new features of the tests,
with study tips on every type of question.

Faster:
Our books cover exactly what you need to
know for the test. No more, no less.

SparkNotes Guide to the SAT & PSAT
SparkNotes Guide to the SAT & PSAT — Deluxe Internet Edition
SparkNotes Guide to the ACT
SparkNotes Guide to the ACT — Deluxe Internet Edition
SparkNotes Guide to the SAT II Writing
SparkNotes Guide to the SAT II U.S. History
SparkNotes Guide to the SAT II Math Ic
SparkNotes Guide to the SAT II Math IIc
SparkNotes Guide to the SAT II Biology
SparkNotes Guide to the SAT II Physics

SparkNotes Study Guides: